DECORATING

WALLS & FLOORS

DECORATING
WALLS & FLOORS

THUNDER BAY
P·R·E·S·S

San Diego, California

Thunder Bay Press
An imprint of the Advantage Publishers Group
5880 Oberlin Drive, San Diego, CA 92121-4794
www.thunderbaybooks.com

© 2003 by Rockport Publishers, Inc.

All notations of errors or omissions should be addressed to Thunder Bay
Press, Editorial Department, at the above address. All other correspon-
dence (author inquiries, permissions) concerning the content of this book
should be addressed to Rockport Publishers, Inc. 33 Commercial Street,
Gloucester, MA 01930-5089. Telephone: (978) 283-9590; Fax: (978)
283-2742; www.rockpub.com.

ISBN 1-59223-036-9

Library of Congress Cataloging-in-Publication Data available upon
request.

Grateful acknowledgment is given to Liz Risney Manning for her work
from *The New Wallpaper Book* on pages 10–153 and 282–285; to Regina
Cole for her work from *The New Flooring Idea Book* on pages 156–245
and 286–299; and to Karen Aude for her work from *Sophisticated Surfaces*
on pages 248–281 and 300–301.

Cover Images: Randy McCaffery, top; Lanny Provo, bottom

Printed in China

1 2 3 4 5 07 06 05 04 03

Contents

Wallpaper

1

From Wallpaper to Wallcovering

HISTORICALLY, wallpaper was just that—paper to cover the walls. Bearing intricate designs and images, often flavored with a hint of the exotic Far East, these papers were laboriously printed using hand-carved blocks or designs made on silk screens onto which inks were brushed, to create the motifs.

The process was expensive and thus most papers were within the means of only the affluent. As with practically all other types of interior furnishings, the Industrial Revolution introduced methods of mass production. A greater number of rolls could be printed and a wider range of patterns made available at less expense, encouraging the use of wallpaper in middle-class homes—the general public, as it were.

The popularity of wallpaper increased, but drawbacks remained. It was, after all, *paper*; difficult to hang because of a tendency to tear, and easily damaged by grease and soil. Glues were inferior by today's standards, creating uneven adhesion and making the paper difficult to remove.

While advancements were made to overcome these shortcomings, the paint industry was making giant strides in research and development. Beginning around 1940 and through the 1950s, the general public preferred to paint their walls. One reason was, curiously enough, disease prevention. One has only to look at advertisements of that era to see how heavily promoted disinfectants were, and painted walls could be periodically washed with such disinfecting solutions. Wallpaper, on the other hand, was not only old-fashioned but seemed to harbor the possibility of germs and contagion—hardly the sort of thing a modern family wanted on its walls. As the popularity of paint increased, the use of wallpaper decreased.

When, in the 1960s, the approval of wallpaper began once again to rise, it did so with gusto. Suddenly, it seems, interior decorators and homeowners could browse through wallpaper selection books to find a large selection of patterns reflecting contemporary designs, executed in trendy colors. These new wallpapers were coated in vinyl, a type of plastic that offered washability. The technology advanced so that instead of just coating the paper, wallcovering was made completely of vinyl. Public reaction was favorable. These new printed rolls of vinyl afforded not only washable surfaces but elements of design in kitchens and bathrooms. Inspired decorators found the alternative to painted walls that had proved too plain and boring to be used throughout the entire home. Printed murals had a resurgence, while additional contemporary materials became available. To compensate for low lighting in small spaces like powder rooms, reflective Mylars were introduced. These new wall coverings weren't made of paper any more, and frankly "wallpaper" had a dated connotation. *Wallcoverings* seemed to flow into the lexicon—a new word for a fresh concept.

Today, members of the industry, as well as interior designers, rarely use the word *wallpaper*. Many homeowners, however, do—so either word is quite acceptable. Both terms have been used in this book; the choice is based on what seemed most appropriate or understandable.

Types of Wallcoverings

The following is a brief description of the most popular types of wallcoverings.

COURTESY OF BARNABY PRINTS, INC. CUSTOM PRINTING

WASHABLE
wallcovering can withstand occasional sponging with a mild detergent solution. Useful for living room or bedroom.

•

SCRUBBABLE
wallcovering can withstand scrubbing with a brush and a mild detergent solution. Useful for kitchen and bath.

•

ABRASION RESISTANT
refers to its ability to withstand rubbing, scrubbing, or scraping. Useful for hallways.

•

STAIN RESISTANT
describes no appreciable change in appearance after removal of different types of stains such as grease, butter, beverages and so on.

•

COLORFASTNESS
is the attribute of resisting change or loss of color caused by exposure to light. Most of today's wallcoverings are colorfast.

•

PREPASTED
is wallcovering with a backing that has been treated with an adhesive easily activated by water.

PEELABLE
means that the top layer of the wallcovering can be dry-peeled away from its backing. This leaves a film of adhered paper that can be used as a liner for hanging a new wallcovering, or can be removed with water. Peelable wallcoverings are usually paperbacked vinyls.

•

STRIPPABLE
means that the wallcovering can be dry-stripped from the wall, leaving a minimum of paste or adhesive residue, without damage to the wall.

FABRIC-BACKED
has a top layer of vinyl and an undersurface of fiberglass or cheesecloth. Most are scrubbable and usually strippable. These are more moisture and grease resistant than other types and less likely to tear; they're also heavy, so are usually not prepasted. When backed with cheesecloth, it tends to have some texture, which is ideal for hiding surface imperfections. Fiberglass-backed vinyls often have a smoother surface.

•

PAPERBACKED VINYL
has a top layer of vinyl and an undersurface of paper (rather than fabric). It is washable and often peelable. It is lighter than the fabric-backed and usually prepasted.

•

VINYL-COATED PAPER
is wallcovering that has been coated with a thin layer of vinyl. It looks more like paper than vinyl, which adds some sophistication. It can usually withstand light washing. It needs to be handled with care when being hung due to a tendency to tear.

•

SPECIALTY WALLCOVERINGS
include embossed, flocked, and textured wallcoverings, as well as murals, grass cloth, and Mylar.

SOLID PAPERS

can be very inexpensive or very costly. They have no vinyl protection, which means cleaning must be done with great care.

•

CUSTOM AND HANDPRINTED WALLCOVERINGS

require attention to detail when lining up the motif of the pattern. Each motif is diligently applied to the paper by skilled craftspeople, using carved blocks or silk screens. Where silk screens are used, the ink is applied to create a different color in the design. The quality of handprinted paper is unmistakable. Handprinted designs may be historical, perhaps even documented, as with the conservation or reproduction of a wallpaper pattern used in a historical building. Or they may be created to coordinate or match the print of a fabric. Internationally recognized design firms such as Brunschwig & Fils and Colefax & Fowler regularly employ handprint wallpaper shops to create their distinctive patterns.

PRECEDING SPREAD: *Even on rainy days, a kitchen with lemon yellow and white wallpaper gives the feeling of sunshine pouring in.* IMPERIAL WALLCOVERINGS

LEFT: *A yellow accent is picked up by the enamel cups in the cabinet.* VILLAGE

BELOW: *Historical restorations may inspire wallcovering designs. The paper in the background is reminiscent of old pewter and worn tavern tables.* IMPERIAL WALLCOVERINGS

The beauty of porcelain jardinieres is captured in this dramatic border, which serves to separate coordinating wallcovering patterns. A collection of blue and white porcelain is displayed against the smaller pattern. GRAMERCY

ABOVE: *Large patterns help fill the space nicely in older homes, where ceilings are likely to be high.* IMPERIAL WALLCOVERINGS

ABOVE RIGHT: *A tranquil pattern for a restful room.* GRAMERCY

FACING PAGE: *The interior designer used the principle of unbroken space to visually enlarge this small, charming bedroom.* GRAMERCY

LEFT: *A dynamic continuity occurs when adjoining rooms are decorated with harmonious, not "matching," wallcovering patterns.* VILLAGE

BELOW: *A large wallcovering pattern adds a lively feeling to this elegant dining room.* DEBORAH BROUGHTON

FACING PAGE: *In this kitchen area, the pattern used for the lower half of the dining room has been repeated—a repetition the eye perceives as pleasing.* GRAMERCY

FACING PAGE: *Blue and white stripes are ideally suited for the bathroom in this beachside home.* VILLAGE

RIGHT: *Deep-colored patterns create a feeling of coziness in this study. Touches of black and gold in the decor complement this striking wallcovering pattern.* GRAMERCY

LEFT: *The fashion industry provided an inspiration for this timeless wallcovering pattern, which features women dressed in Dior gowns—ideal for a dressing room.* GRAMERCY

BELOW: *Perfectly matched trim enamel is a crisp accent to any wallcovering; in this case, Wedgwood blue was chosen for door, trim, molding, and little round table found at a flea market.* SANDERSON

RIGHT: *Use a favorite piece of furniture, such as this blue-painted chair, for inspiration in choosing wallpaper patterns. The well-balanced floral patterns of this dining room show the type of creative details one can expect when using a professional designer.* GRAMERCY

FACING PAGE: *A pattern this size is wonderfully proportioned for this gracious living room.* GRAMERCY

2

Sensational Style

A WELL-DECORATED ROOM with coordinating wallcoverings,
borders, and fabrics is no longer a luxury few can afford, nor need it be
a time-consuming effort of search and despair.

A wonderful world of decorating freedom has emerged. No longer is using stripes and prints together likely to produce raised eyebrows. One can even throw plaid fabrics into the mix. What makes it work? Primarily, color coordination. When the same colors are in the stripe, print, and plaid, interior style *works*.

One need not have the finely honed instincts of an interior designer to create striking style. Wallcovering companies have made coordinating easy by mixing and matching suggested patterns for you. As you leaf through their selection books, you will find colorful pages showing rooms in which coordinating prints have been applied on walls and ceilings, followed by samples of the actual wallcoverings used. These selection books can give an inspiring look at how to work with various patterns. Oftentimes, fabrics that match are available, adding to the wide range of customized interiors one can realize. A local seamstress can produce a stunning window treatment to mix with or match the patterns you select; coordinated comforters and bed linens can be created; and an upholstery shop can revamp existing furniture into stylish "new" pieces by recovering them with a fabric that echoes the pattern used on the walls or elsewhere in the room.

It is possible to create your own coordinated decor. While browsing through wallcovering selection books, look for the same color within the patterns, or colors of different *values* from within the same color family. Value refers to the lightness or darkness of a color achieved by tinting or shading. A *tint* is achieved by adding **white**, while a *shade* is achieved by adding **black** to a given color. For a good example of this concept, take a look at the strips of gradational colors available in paint stores. The lightest tinted color is at the top, while the deepest shaded color is at the bottom. Using a tint and a shade, one as dominant and the other as an accent or trim color, will result in good color coordination. Use the same principle of color value to guide you in selecting wallcovering patterns.

Mixed and matched wallcoverings can be used with one pattern on the upper half of a wall and the other on the lower half with a wooden chair rail or a wallcovering border to separate the patterns. Or use a dominant pattern on three walls with a coordinated pattern on the fourth. A dormered room can be papered with a dark background pattern on its walls and the same pattern, but in reverse (oftentimes available), within the dormers. The lighter reverse background will produce more reflected light.

The Feeling of Color

Here, color is broken down into families based around the same basic hue.

THE *RED* FAMILY

HUES
pink, rose, cardinal, raspberry, burgundy, maroon

CHARACTERISTICS
warmest of all colors, advancing, cheerful, active, stimulating, bold, vital, dramatic, exciting

EFFECT
A red room appears smaller by bringing the background closer; red objects appear larger because red focuses attention; red brings warmth and excitement to a cool room.

PRECAUTION
Too much red is overly exciting.

FAST FACT
A red room stimulates appetite.

·

THE *ORANGE* FAMILY

HUES
peach, coral, pumpkin, copper, terra-cotta, rust, warm brown

CHARACTERISTICS
welcoming, cheerful, warm, glowing, advancing, friendly

EFFECT
Much like the red family but to a lesser degree; in soft tints is a good color mixer; a good choice for kitchens and family rooms.

PRECAUTION
Like red, can be overwhelming if overused.

FAST FACT
Orange rooms tend to make people tire more easily.

THE *YELLOW* FAMILY

HUES
cream, straw, lemon, canary, gold, tan, tobacco

CHARACTERISTICS
warm, luminous, radiant, classic, expansive, accepting

EFFECT
Yellow rooms appear brighter and lighter because of the color's reflective quality; can be used to light up a room without making it feel smaller; a classic kitchen choice.

PRECAUTION
Yellow tints and tones need to be tested under artificial light as they appear different in various kinds of light.

FAST FACT
Babies tend to cry more and children are more argumentative in yellow nurseries than in pink, baby blue, or pale green rooms.

·

THE *GREEN* FAMILY

HUES
mint, lettuce, pea, grass, sea, olive, bottle, forest

CHARACTERISTICS
refreshing, cool, receding, restful

EFFECT
In lighter shades, a room will seem larger because the wall seems further away; brings atmosphere of relaxation to room; important hue where restfulness is important; most friendly with all other colors.

PRECAUTION
May make a room with a northern exposure feel cold.

FAST FACT
Green is least tiring to the eyes, which is the reason accountants' shades and surgeons' traditional scrubs are green.

·

THE *BLUE* FAMILY

HUES
baby, powder, sky, turquoise, royal, navy, midnight

CHARACTERISTICS
coolest of all colors, most receding, much-loved hue, serene

EFFECT
Blue room appears cooler than if painted with a warm hue; makes a room feel more airy and spacious; makes objects look smaller and more distant; makes whites appear more luminescent.

PRECAUTION
Can be depressing in dull shades.

FAST FACT
People associate stability and leadership with the color blue; important documents are often bound in blue.

THE *VIOLET* FAMILY

HUES

orchid, lavender, mauve, violet, purple, plum

CHARACTERISTICS

impressive hue; creates quiet feeling atmosphere

EFFECT

Dark tones make objects appear formal and rich; transitional color—feels cool when mixed with blue and warm when mixed with red; meditative.

PRECAUTION

Strong shades can be overpowering.

FAST FACT

In medieval times, only royalty was allowed to wear purple.

PRECEDING SPREAD: *As minimalism becomes more popular, we are likely to see patterns that fit the look.* IMPERIAL WALLCOVERINGS

ABOVE: *Older homes often have interesting architectural details such as the arched window and the built-in cabinet beside the fireplace. This appropriate wallcovering captures the spirit of the early twentieth century.* GRAMERCY

BELOW: *A traditional foyer sets the tone for a home. Don't be afraid to use rich colors; this red, for example, suggests warmth and cheerfulness.* SCHUMACHER

LEFT: *In this authentic bath, a botanical print wallcovering was used. Botanical prints were popular in the early part of this century. Good reproductions, such as this pedestal sink and footed bathtub, are now available for those wishing to capture the look.* GRAMERCY

BELOW: *A different pattern of wallcovering helps to differentiate the alcove space from the rest of the room.* SEABROOK WALLCOVERINGS

ABOVE: *Although we often associate red with oriental motifs, this blue with a subtle fish design works wonderfully with the decor.* GRAMERCY

RIGHT: *A very charming eating area with a great deal of coordination. Everything matches to create a harmonious mood.* HARLEQUIN— DISTRIBUTED BY WHITTAKER & WOODS

FACING PAGE: *This morning glory pattern was a good choice as background to the bird house collection.* SEABROOK WALLCOVERINGS

LEFT: *A simple, Regency-inspired interior in which the crispness of blue and white have been used for a chic effect.* HARLEQUIN– DISTRIBUTED BY WHITTAKER & WOODS

ABOVE: *In this child's room, the polka-dotted headboard was painted to match the whimsical border, in which bears skate around the room.* VILLAGE

ABOVE: *Good coordination creates a charming decor in this attic bedroom retreat. The fabric colors match even though the prints are different.* SANDERSON

ABOVE: *A strong design, but beautifully implemented, in this large and interesting bath.*
GRAMERCY

LEFT: *A great example of a room in which fabrics and wallcoverings match in color but not in pattern. The exception is the window treatment, created from wallcovering-matched fabric.*
GRAMERCY

LEFT: *A boldly coordinated bath that features a sumptuously curtained tub.* DECORATING DEN INTERIORS

BELOW: *A linear look is emphasized by the wallcovering pattern, which complements the furnishings, floor mosaic, and glass panel adjoining the door.* IMPERIAL WALLCOVERINGS

FACING PAGE: *A straightforward woven pattern is a great starting point for a sparse, eclectic interior.* IMPERIAL WALLCOVERINGS

ABOVE AND FACING PAGE: *A retro 1950s look in this loft apartment benefits from a complementary background. The patterns in these two photos demonstrate how well the selections worked.* IMPERIAL WALLCOVERINGS

FACING PAGE: *A French country look has been achieved with this simple, yet elegant, striped wallpaper.* IMPERIAL WALLCOVERINGS

RIGHT: *This dining room gloriously combines the tropical with the traditional. The effect is paradoxical—a sort of relaxed grandeur.* GRAMERCY

BELOW: *A Fabergé egg collection print that is nothing less than stunning. By repeating the pattern in fabric details—the chair, ottoman, and pillow—the decorating efforts could be considered flawless.* GRAMERCY

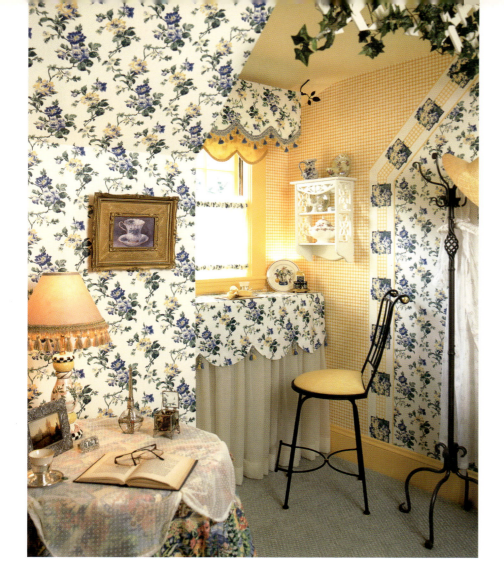

LEFT: *An ingenious use of wallcovering and borders create an "alcove" in this country design.* DECORATING DEN INTERIORS

BELOW: *A painted pink ceiling softly offsets this lovely French country-style bedroom. The exquisite pattern on paper and fabric is a custom design.* BRUNSCHWIG & FILS

FACING PAGE: *A draped bed and matched fabrics, wallcoverings, and borders combine to create a room of sensationally coordinated style.* GRAMERCY

ABOVE: *A border defines this sweet, pleasantly coordinated nursery.*
DECORATING DEN INTERIORS

RIGHT: *The coordinating fabric to this wallcovering pattern was used for bedding.* SEABROOK WALLCOVERINGS

FACING PAGE: *This comfortable print, used throughout this small room, actually makes the room look larger than if different patterns were used.* BRUNSCHWIG & FILS

ABOVE: *Wallcovering may mimic a painted finish, as in this subtle selection that looks sponge-painted.* DECORATING DEN INTERIORS

RIGHT: *Softness is conveyed by this country-influenced room, from the upholstered screen to the sheer drapes. The starting point is the pale, light-on-light wallcovering.* GRAMERCY

FACING PAGE: *A distinctive border helps create the elegant ease of this room.* SCHUMACHER

LEFT: *A charming pattern for a charming room. This room in a mother-in-law's suite functions as a multipurpose room. What better way to enjoy family activities than in this cheerful setting.* GRAMERCY

FACING PAGE: *An obvious choice for a bathroom, and a fun one as well. The coordinating border in front of the base cabinet is a nice touch.*
SEABROOK WALLCOVERINGS

ABOVE: *Soft neutrals create this subued eclectic setting.* DECORATING DEN INTERIORS

FACING PAGE: *This elegant, detailed wallcovering sets up the restrained aesthetic of this perfectly coordinated off-white bedroom.* IMPERIAL WALLCOVERINGS

ABOVE: *This entryway encourages its occupants to be ever ready when it comes to a walkabout. The strong colors in the wide border print of mallards, sunflowers, and pottery stand out against the more subdued striped wallcovering on the wall.* YORK WALLCOVERINGS

RIGHT: *Theme-ing a room refers to repeating the dominant theme. In this case, a backdrop of tied flies used for fly fishing is picked up with the border print and the decorative accessories in the room.*
YORK WALLCOVERINGS

FACING PAGE: *Vaulted ceilings are dramatic but this one is made even more so with the use of a simulated cork ceiling. The effect makes the room feel cozier.*
YORK WALLCOVERINGS

3

Looking Up: Ceiling Style

TODAY, ceilings are often untapped design areas with which to complement your decor. This has not always been the case. Where once artistic plaster medallions took center stage and richly carved ceiling moldings framed the perimeter of a room, plain blank ceilings, usually white, have become the norm.

As the skills and talents of Old World craftsmen died off, so did the prominence of ceiling details.

The re-introduction of architectural elements in modern materials such as cast resin and vinyl-coated Styrofoam, have inspired wallcovering companies to respond by depicting such details on easily applied wallpaper. Many of today's wallcovering books feature these ceiling medallion and trim patterns, to the delight of the decorator. If the desired medallions are not available, an ingenious decorator can create them by cutting out a motif from a large wallcovering pattern.

When more than a medallion is desired to draw the eye upward, the entire ceiling area can be covered with either the same pattern used on the walls, or a coordinating pattern. When the ceiling is covered with the same pattern, the room will actually appear larger. By downplaying contrast, small areas actually look larger. This is a visual phenomenon decorators often take advantage of. Papering a small bedroom with the same wallcovering pattern on ceiling and walls will make the room appear larger than if the ceiling were painted, or if different patterns had been used above and below the chair rail.

Trim borders can be applied to the perimeter of the ceiling to strengthen visual interest. The corners should be planned so that they adjoin each other at about the same detail in the pattern of the border and cut at a miter. This technique helps to achieve a professional look.

Papering a large ceiling can be intimidating for the do-it-yourselfer. Thoughts of a sticky strip spiraling downward while moving from one end of the room to the other can put a damper on enthusiasm. It is difficult to climb up and down a ladder, pushing it forward while trying to maintain pressure on the ceiling strip being applied. If hanging wall covering on a ceiling is a first attempt, a small bathroom ceiling might prove enough of a challenge; an extra pair of hands and an encouraging word will be welcome additions. Ladders that fold to create a scaffold help ease some of the problems. Of course, when one is looking for effect as opposed to experience, hiring a professional to paper the ceiling is a reasonable option. Papering the ceiling is a decorating technique that adds interior interest all through the house.

Making the Most of Medallions

When a medallion is
desired as a base for an existing chandelier,
its position on the ceiling is easily determined. In a
room without a centered chandelier or light fixture, the
decorator measures the ceiling to find a position equidis-
tant from its side walls. Rectangular rooms are as good a
candidate for a ceiling medallion as square rooms. For
long, narrow ceilings, as in a hall, a series of medallions
can be used. Generally, an odd number such as three or
five is more effective than an even number. It may prove
visually pleasing to use a larger medallion in the center
with smaller ones on either side, or in a case where five
medallions are to be used, to rotate from
small to large to small again.

PRECEDING SPREAD: *A suspended light fixture is greatly enhanced by the large ceiling medallion, suggestive of antique plasterwork once created by skilled craftsmen. Along the ceiling is a diecut medallion border. On the walls, corners are graced with Corinthian columns, adding a Greek Revival flavor to the room.* EISENHART WALLCOVERINGS

ABOVE: *Bathroom ceilings, which are generally smaller than most rooms, can be encouraging to the do-it-yourself paperhanger.* YORK WALLCOVERINGS

FACING PAGE: *This coffered ceiling allowed for a border to be used as an inset. The result is very dramatic.* EISENHART WALLCOVERINGS

RIGHT: *Here, a plaid pattern perfectly complements the ruggedness of ceiling timber beams.* VILLAGE

ABOVE: *A blue and white gingham pattern on the ceiling emphasizes the country feeling in this eating area. The look is completed with the use of matching fabric on the chair cushions.* WARNER WALLCOVERINGS

LEFT: *Painting the slope of the dormer ceiling to match the walls was an option, but papering it continued the pattern flow. The border accentuates its height.* WARNER WALLCOVERINGS

FACING PAGE: *Children love to be totally surrounded by color and images. This young water lover enjoys staring at the manatees swimming beneath the sky canopy.* WARNER WALLCOVERINGS

ABOVE: *This rather masculine effect is achieved with two linear patterns, one on the ceiling and the other on the walls. A shade of red is the dominant hue throughout.* GRAMERCY

LEFT: *A French country look is achieved by using this rich blue paper between the exposed weathered beams of this spacious bath.* GRAMERCY

FACING PAGE: *This evocative room includes a faux finish wallcovering pattern on the ceiling, which provides a mellow candlelit feeling.* GRAMERCY

FACING PAGE: *The plaid ceiling adds a touch of country to this hospitable dining room. The distinctive pattern on the opposite wall was created by stacking a border pattern.* VILLAGE

RIGHT: *The mottled look of this ceiling wallcovering is in keeping with the rich architectural details of the window and moldings.* GRAMERCY

BELOW: *Here is a perfect example of using strong colors to create impact. The austerity a high ceiling can give is totally diminished by the warmth of the deep red-based paper. Building a soffit around its perimeter provides another opportunity to add wonderful detail. By papering between ceiling beams, this farm house detail is accentuated. The whole effect complements the richness of the room's furnishings.* GRAMERCY

ABOVE: *It is not unusual to find small and large sizes of a coordinated motif. Here, the ceiling benefits from the larger, more open scale, while the walls are papered in the more condensed version.* SUNWORTHY WALLCOVERINGS

FACING PAGE: *The ceiling in this older home was beginning to show its age. A liner paper was applied to seal and smooth the surface, then this restful pattern was used to give the ceiling an attractive finish.*
WARNER WALLCOVERINGS

FACING PAGE: *A grass cloth paper was applied to this elegant bed-room ceiling. With grass cloth, real grasses are woven onto a backing, and unlike traditional wallcoverings, the paste is applied to the surface of the ceiling.* GRAMERCY

BELOW: *A classic example of using stripes and checks together, in a fresh blue and white color combination.* SUNWORTHY WALLCOVERINGS

LEFT: *This ceiling pattern is subtle, so as not to distract from the skylight, but to highlight its presence, the border was added. Skylights are appreciated for the ability to brighten a room by shedding natural light.*
EISENHART WALLCOVERINGS

BELOW: *Want the feeling of being surrounded by lush green foliage? In this room you would feel like the trees have formed an overhead canopy.* BRUNSCHWIG & FILS

FACING PAGE: *This vaulted ceiling was dramatic but lacked distinction, particularly with the rich, dark green walls. By covering the ceiling with an airy pattern, the room comes into focus.* DECORATING DEN INTERIORS

ABOVE: *This ceiling pattern, with its shaded "dimensional" medallions, resembles an old plaster or pressed-tin ceiling.* YORK WALLCOVERINGS

FACING PAGE: *The same pattern in blacks and greys gives the medallions more definition. You can see the effect color has by this comparison.* YORK WALLCOVERINGS

ABOVE: *Available now are "corners," which allow you to tie the border together, as in this ceiling corner. This helps overcome the problem of mismatching pattern motifs.* YORK WALLCOVERINGS

FACING PAGE: *A daybed, draped from a papered ceiling, is a dramatic focal point to this room.* YORK WALLCOVERINGS

4

Border Lines

THERE IS a strong correlation between the growth in popularity of the new wallcoverings and the upswing in the market for border patterns. As recently as a decade ago, few border patterns were available; what was available was used largely in place of ceiling moldings or to create a chair rail effect on walls.

Intrepid interior designers, in reaction against the stereotypical, began using borders in unexpected ways. They placed borders at any height, including the top edge of baseboard moldings. They outlined windows to create more definition. They used borders, not in place of rich carved crown moldings, but in addition to them. Two different patterns of borders might be used within the same room. Interior design magazines, quick to pick up on trends, began to focus on these creative border uses, and as consumer demand for new borders exploded, the wallcovering industry responded.

Before their popularity, borders were printed almost as an afterthought. The designs were fairly standard—a rope, a ribbon, a garland of flowers, or a twist of ivy, generic enough to add a decorative touch to most available wallcovering patterns. Today, however, the wallcovering industry tends to design the border *first*; they are following the lead of interior designers, who are likely to choose a border first, use it as a theme, then select a wallcovering pattern to match.

The nonprofessional home decorator has found numerous uses for borders. Those who gravitate toward painting a room will add a border as a decorative touch, admittedly much easier than papering an entire room. Creative do-it-yourselfers who add a faux finish to a paint job with a sponge or use the rag rolling technique, might incorporate a border to disguise the unevenness where the wall meets the ceiling.

Since borders are so often used in rooms that are painted or papered with a nearly solid color design, the use of color and its powerful visual and emotional impact is a tool worthy of understanding. Color has a tremendous influence on our lives. Understanding some basic theories will help you harness the power of color.

There are three primary colors: red, yellow, and blue. When two of these colors are mixed together, they create one of the three secondary colors: orange (red and yellow), green (yellow and blue), and violet (blue and red). These six colors are often arranged on a wheel to help in demonstrating color theory. The red, orange, and yellow half of the wheel feels warm and appears to come forward or advance. The green, blue, and violet hues feel cool and appear to recede.

Select any hue, and its color opposite on the wheel would be called its *complementary* (or contrasting) color: The basic complementary pairs are red and green, orange and blue, yellow and violet. Complementary colors used as the basis for a decorating scheme have a significant impact—imagine red and green side by side. Complementary color schemes need to be used with caution, for it is easy to overdo the effect. Colors that are side by side on the color wheel are referred to as *analogous* (or related) colors. These are the easiest colors to use harmoniously and, therefore, are the most popular. When tints or tones of the same color are used, the scheme is called *monochromatic*.

Finding Your Own Theme

A practice called "theme-ing" is another way of coordinating a room's decor. In this case, the style of a room is produced by using wallcoverings with a dominant motif or a theme, enhanced perhaps with an accentuating border, and then choosing related accessories. Usually the theme reflects the owner's interest. It's amazing that wallcovering companies have managed to design patterns representing so many different hobbies. A well-stocked wallcovering retailer is bound to offer access to prints reflecting *your* interests. This interior features the pineapple, a symbol of hospitality, as a design motif. Though the choice of styles or themes is endless, some popular styles include Asian or international, Victorian, country, and eclectic.

PRECEDING SPREAD: *This subtle border enhances the look of solid furnishings.*
GRAMERCY

RIGHT: *The latest borders are diecut or laser cut around the edge of the design. The eye appreciates the graceful curved effect.* VILLAGE

BELOW: *This whimsical border design reflects the spirit of the room. Borders are oftentimes selected first with a wallcovering to match as the secondary consideration.*
IMPERIAL WALLCOVERINGS

LEFT: *The gracefulness of this curved swag and floral border is a dynamic counterbalance to the linear striped pattern on either side of the bed.* VILLAGE

BELOW: *A traditional use of a border, where wall meets ceiling. This pattern helps bring the garden into the kitchen.* GRAMERCY

FACING PAGE: *Sometimes dividing the same pattern used above and below a molding looks static, creating the need for a border.* VILLAGE

ABOVE: *This border can be personalized with the initial of one's surname.* JOLIE PAPIER

FACING PAGE: *In this music room, the border is large and dominant, giving it its rightful sense of importance in the sparsely furnished space.* GRAMERCY

LEFT: *This border gives a beach house bath-room a sun-drenched appeal.*
IMPERIAL WALLCOVERINGS

FACING PAGE: *Kids adore the stimulating primary colors used in this children's pattern.*
SEABROOK WALLCOVERINGS

FACING PAGE: *The nautical theme is a popular one among sailors. The knot pattern on the wall under the stairs is used again on the opposite wall (not shown) where a collection of pond boats has been hung.* GRAMERCY

ABOVE: *Among quilters and those who love the country look, patchwork hearts symbolize love that endures.*
IMPERIAL WALLCOVERINGS

FACING PAGE: *Bedrooms benefit from the more vibrant colors added with wallcoverings. When you wake up in this room, you feel suddenly energized.*

HARLEQUIN—DISTRIBUTED BY
WHITTAKER & WOODS

BELOW: *As the popularity of topiary grows so do prints that contain such specimens. And what to use as a border? It appears this oak leaf and pine bough print does a nice enough job.*

SEABROOK WALLCOVERINGS

RIGHT: *The fruits of the gardener's labor appear in this kitchen. Oftentimes, it is a color within the border that suggests what to use elsewhere. The countertop takes its cue from the eggplant in the print.* WARNER WALLCOVERINGS

FACING PAGE: *This elephant border is a perfect accompaniment to the hand-carved dining room table and African sculpture.* GRAMERCY

TOP RIGHT: *Look closely and you will see how the border was cut to create individual panels beneath the chair rail.*
EISENHART WALLCOVERINGS

ABOVE: *A shells and starfish border complement a shell collection in this waterfront home.* SEABROOK WALLCOVERINGS

FACING PAGE: *Adjoining the kitchen is this charming dining area where a rustic border has been used above the alcove ceiling and again at a mid-section of the dining room.*
WARNER WALLCOVERINGS

LEFT: *Here the border frames the window and the fireplace wall to add a decorative touch to an already well-appointed bedroom.* EISENHART WALLCOVERINGS

BELOW LEFT: *Molding accentuates the border and its placement above this attractive desk.* WARNER WALLCOVERINGS

FACING PAGE: *Borders that are sculptured resemble the natural hang of a ribbon or fabric swag.* WARNER WALLCOVERINGS

ABOVE : *This is a good example of both a sculptured border and a straight-cut border used together.*
WARNER WALLCOVERINGS

FACING PAGE : *A laser-cut border adds superb detail to this country-influenced bathroom.*
WARNER WALLCOVERINGS

LEFT: *The fabric design inspired the matching border print, used effectively in this room off the center hall.* WARNER OF LONDON— DISTRIBUTED BY WHITTAKER & WOODS

FACING PAGE: *Here, the charm is in the details: The panel effect below the chair rail, the centered fabric design on all parts of the chair covers, the clever window treatment, the green bow over the clock, and the matching swag border create a totally enchanting environment.* WARNER OF LONDON—DISTRIBUTED BY WHITTAKER & WOODS

LEFT: *This large kitchen has been updated by using a stylish, wide border pattern.*
SEABROOK WALLCOVERINGS

BELOW: *A contemporary look can be carried throughout the house by choosing similar patterns.* SEABROOK DESIGNS

FACING PAGE: *A bold pattern helped transform this hallway. Again, this primitive design border can be hung vertically as well as horizontally.*
SEABROOK WALLCOVERINGS

LEFT: *A softly colored border gives an Impressionistic effect in this kitchen.*
SEABROOK WALLCOVERINGS

BELOW: *An architectural detail border has been used in a room where people gather to play afternoon bridge.* YORK WALLCOVERINGS

FACING PAGE: *This avid gardener found the right border for her indoor potting shed.*
VILLAGE

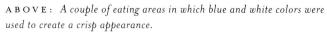

ABOVE: *A couple of eating areas in which blue and white colors were used to create a crisp appearance.*

LEFT, VILLAGE; RIGHT, IMPERIAL WALLCOVERINGS

FACING PAGE: *This sculptured border reinforces the traditional look of this room.* WARNER WALLCOVERINGS

LEFT: *A peek into a kitchen, carried through with the same paper used in the dining area. To help set it apart, a matching border was used.* VILLAGE

BELOW: *The reverse treatment, that of using a border in the dining room and not the kitchen, is seen in this setting.* VILLAGE

FACING PAGE: *This large pattern gains restraint from the smaller sized complementary border.* GRAMERCY

LEFT: *A white bathroom is a clean, pure, contemporary choice. This subtle border serves to enhance, not overwhelm.*
IMPERIAL WALLCOVERINGS

BELOW: *This pale border and wallcovering pattern nicely offsets the combination of dark wood and gleaming porcelain.*
GRAMERCY

FACING PAGE: *Floral patterns have always been popular, and give a delightful period feeling to this border.*
SEABROOK WALLCOVERINGS

ABOVE: *For a gardener's kitchen, an herb-patterned border echoes the real thing.*
WARNER WALLCOVERINGS

FACING PAGE: *The viewer's eye can spot the repetitive element in this decor. The bottom of this border has been cut to create realism in this fern motif.* VILLAGE

LEFT: *Another contemporary border—colorful hanging quilt blocks that suggest warm informality.* IMPERIAL WALLCOVERINGS

BELOW: *A great example of how to treat wallcoverings when a trim or molding shifts in height.* SUNWORTHY WALLCOVERINGS

FACING PAGE: *The inspiration for this wallcovering motif is a collection of Staffordshire figures.* HARLEQUIN— DISTRIBUTED BY WHITTAKER & WOODS

ABOVE: *When borders are used at this height, the eye is automatically lifted when entering the room. In this case, what the eye sees is a collection suggestive of the occupant's interests.*
SUNWORTHY WALLCOVERINGS

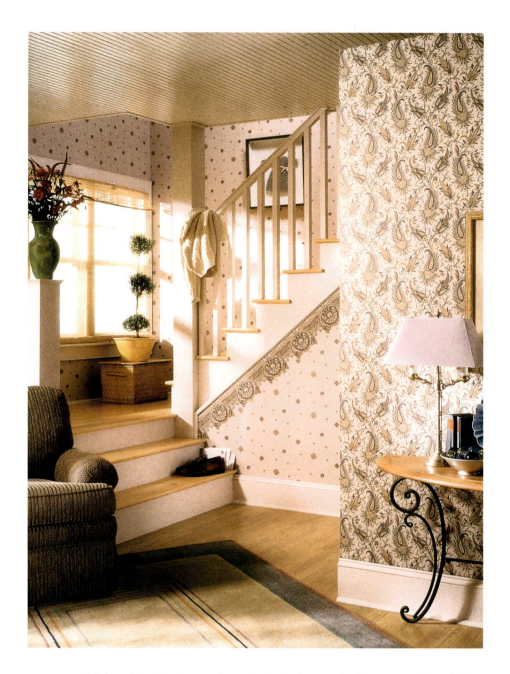

A B O V E : *A light and airy interior came from exposing the bare wooden floors, using white paint for the ceiling and trim, and using a decorative border to add detail under the stairs.*

SUNWORTHY WALLCOVERINGS

5

Finishing Touches

JUST AS JEWELRY, a belt, or a hat tilted over one eye adds distinction to a plain black dress, complementary accessories and creative details add panache to a room—often the defining difference between good and great decorating.

The eye is quick to catch repeat elements of design; so accessories that match in pattern or color add to the ultimate style of a room. The most obvious choice for capturing this effect with wallcoverings is to use fabric with a matching print for pillows, curtains, tiebacks, and upholstered pieces. A fairly easy approach to adding a matching or coordinating detail to a room is to paper the inside of cabinets or bookshelves within the room. Small pieces of wallcovering are fairly easy to handle. Trimming is the most difficult part; however, the wet paper *gives* as it is fitted to the inside and allows for creasing to mark the excess needing to be cut. The paper can then be pulled away from the surface and trimmed with scissors. Or if it is not too awkward, resort to the traditional method with a straightedge, trimming with a single-sided razor.

Displaying objects to accessorize a room works well and is most effective when they are presented as a collection. For example, five blue bottles of varying sizes, a round blue dish, and one

rectangular blue inkwell grouped together will look far more interesting than any single blue element. Pictures and photos also look best when grouped together. Buy plain, oversized frames and use leftover wallcoverings on the frame border, or use a colored matting to match your walls.

Adding complementary details and accessories to a room creates a cohesive feeling that is pleasing to the eye and makes the room comfortable to be in. A simple approach is to match appropriate colors, textures, and prints. For instance, tiebacks for muslin-type country curtains will catch the eye and reinforce the coordinated effort made. Loosely covering a wastebasket with matching fabric held together with a ribbon is another clever and inexpensive accessory. Small toss pillows add a touch of softness to the decor. There are pillow covers that can be made by simply wrapping and tying fabric around a pillow form. A fabric or craft store will provide patterns for these ideas and more.

Creating Screens

Screens are a particularly easy decorative accessory to make and cover with wallcovering. Solid pieces of smooth wood, or even foamcore framed with wood, can be simply hinged together to create a folding screen. Access to a jigsaw is useful for creating curved screens. Because they are so easy to paper, they can be recovered often.

•

Truly functional accessories, screens help divide space without costly partitions. They provide privacy and create cozy work areas. Screens can be used to hide half-finished projects. Position a small screen to camouflage the look of a black hole when not using your fireplace. Use a shorter screen as a backdrop on a side buffet table.

PRECEDING SPREAD: *The back of a bookcase is an ideal place to add leftover wall-covering. Notice how the china in this hutch is emphasized by papering behind the shelves.* VILLAGE

ABOVE: *Animal prints add a wild, earthy tone to this bedroom.* SUNWORTHY WALLCOVERINGS

LEFT: *The papered background to this nursery room bookshelf turns a dark shelf into playful storage for stuffed animals and toys.* SUNWORTHY WALLCOVERINGS

BELOW: *The folding screen paper picks up the setee's fabric to tie in the decor.* GRAMERCY

FACING PAGE: *In this elegant bedroom, a papered screen covers a dark, empty fireplace with a coordinating floral pattern.* VILLAGE

LEFT: *A covered screen adds a focal point in this bedroom.* VILLAGE

BELOW: *Covered boxes make attractive storage units, especially when the pattern coordinates with the room's wallcovering patterns.* IMPERIAL WALLCOVERINGS

FACING PAGE: *This screen hides a radiator, allows for privacy, and fits in beautifully with the decor.* GRAMERCY

ABOVE: *This spectacular, regal room with
an elegantly draped bed is a triumph of matched
wallcovering and fabric.* BRUNSCHWIG & FILS

FACING PAGE: *This true-blue, traditional room is lightened with a light, narrow
screen.* SUNWORTHY WALLCOVERINGS

ABOVE: *The row-of-houses pattern adds a
clever touch to the wall side of the shelf.*
YORK WALLCOVERINGS

A B O V E : *The dominant ribbon theme of this bathroom is accentuated with the covered boxes on the floor.* YORK WALLCOVERINGS

RIGHT: *A plethora of covered hat boxes makes a lovely collection in and of itself.* VILLAGE

FACING PAGE: *Preparing to cover lamp-shades and other accessories can be fun. Just a few pieces of favorite wallpaper, and adequate glue and tools, are necessary. To create an adjustable lamp shade, punch holes in a strip of pleated wallpaper and string cord through the holes.* VILLAGE

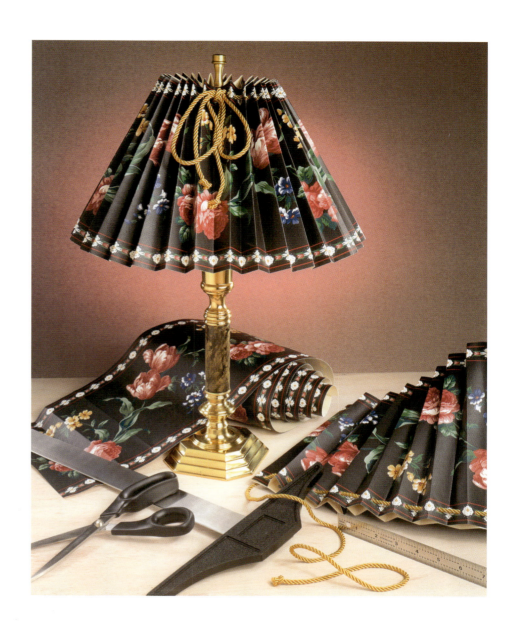

When borders are non–directional, they can be used to frame a wall, a window, or to fill the area within architectural moldings used to create panels. The following photographs help you envision the result if you decide to create such an effect.

ABOVE: *Here, details—architectural or merely textural—are cleverly combined to create a beckoning window seat.* WARNER OF LONDON—
DISTRIBUTED BY WHITTAKER & WOODS

FACING PAGE: *Perfect symmetry and the restraint of just one orchid make this space stunning.* WARNER OF LONDON—
DISTRIBUTED BY WHITTAKER & WOODS

Many of the new laser-cut borders allow the decorator to pull apart sections; virtually all borders have motifs that can be trimmed and cut apart. By applying pieces of border on door panels and over entrances, a distinctive découpage look can be achieved.

ABOVE: SUNWORTHY WALLCOVERINGS

FACING PAGE: VILLAGE

RIGHT: *The latest in wallcovering designs are faux architectural details. One can easily create a framed panel effect, which allows for a number of distinctive, professional-looking effects.* EISENHART WALLCOVERINGS

FACING PAGE: *Curved corners, available with some borders, join straight border pieces to create this elegant fireplace panel.* YORK WALLCOVERINGS

LEFT: *A subtle architectural border is echoed in the mirror frame and columns of a hall table.*
YORK WALLCOVERINGS

FACING PAGE: *Bold ionic columns lend importance and elegance to an entrance hall.*
GRAMERCY

6

Tricks of the Trade

HOW TO SELECT AND HANG WALLPAPER LIKE A PRO

For the do-it-yourselfer who is inspired by
the images of wallcovering in this book, the
following is a guide to decorating your home with
some of those beautiful wallcovering designs. Here you
will find information on selecting a wallcovering for
every room of your home, preparing to hang, hanging
the paper, and addressing wallcovering challenges.
The range and variety of ideas and tips will make
it easier for you to complete your own
wallcovering projects with style.

Selecting a Wallcovering

Selecting a wallcovering pattern is a very personal choice, a subjective matter of one's likes and dislikes. While many people find searching out their "likes" exciting, others can find it time-consuming and confusing. Interior designers, schooled in color matching and design interaction, can be well worth their fees to provide such professional advice. A designer-selected pattern, initially dismissed by a homeowner, often becomes a brilliantly successful design element once hung. Use wallcovering patterns to play off special features of a room, such as dormers. Paper a dormered room with a dark background pattern on its walls and a reverse of the same pattern within the dormers. As a result, the lighter reverse background will generate more reflected light.

Particularly for those choosing their own wallcovering, it is essential to follow steps that could be called Matching, Measuring, and Making Sure.

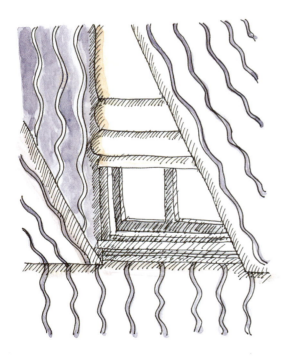

DARK PATTERN ON WALL

MATCHING: Patterns can be plain, resembling a painted finish, have a subtle overall design, or include vertical stripes that produce what is called a "random match." In a random match, there is no design within the pattern that needs to be aligned when hanging these strips. With plaids, checks, foulards, and figures, the overall pattern must be perfectly matched when hanging. The motif will repeat itself at regular intervals. This interval is referred to as a "drop match." The wallcovering selection book will specify the measurement of the drop.

DARK PATTERN ON DORMER

RANDOM MATCH   DROP MATCH

MEASURING: When you are ready to order or purchase your selection, take careful measurements of the room to be papered and allow the retailer to help with the number of rolls needed. They will keep in mind whether your pattern selection is a random match or drop match, the latter requiring more paper as a result of anticipated waste. Count the surfaces that won't be covered: windows, doors, and fireplaces, for example. The square feet or meters of these areas will be deducted from the overall amount needed.

Most U.S. wallcoverings are 18 inches (46 cm) wide and are sold in double rolls, although generally priced in single rolls. Some may be wider but contain shorter lengths. Regardless of the width of the roll, consider there to be 30 usable feet in each U.S. roll, and 8 meters or 24 feet in each European roll.

MAKING SURE: Dye lot match is important. When patterns are produced, a large run is made using the same vat of ink. A popular pattern will be printed repeatedly, each time using a new vat of ink. The colors might change slightly due to pigment saturation of the ink batch, air temperature, humidity of the paper, drying time, or any number of other factors. While this does not affect paper quality nor in any way make it inferior, a color shift could be noticeable. For this reason, it is important to buy the right number of rolls, all bearing the same dye lot numbers, at the start.

A good wallcovering job will last for years with just general care and maintenance. In all probability, you'll tire of the pattern before it actually needs to be replaced.

ABOVE: *Random match pattern.* WARNER

BELOW: *Drop match pattern.* EISENHART

Sampling: The Secret of Successful Style

When selecting a pattern, it's worth ordering a small sample.
Tape it to the wall of the room in which it will be used.

•

The natural, artificial, and reflected light within that particular room will no doubt appear to change a color. You may find you are not as enamored with the paper's color or pattern as you were in the wallcovering shop. Hanging a sample will also give you an opportunity to judge the size of a pattern. Too many times, novice buyers shy away from large prints, opting for smaller ones. This can turn to regret; although the detail can be easily discerned on the pages of a wallcovering selection book, it may become lost once applied to a larger surface. This can be a particularly embarrassing gaffe; for example, papering a boy's bedroom in white paper with a small red fleur-de-lis pattern can seem like a great choice—but the paper may "read" not as red and white but pink!

•

Large designs may look overwhelming on a 12" x 24" (30 cm x 61 cm) page and its drop-match dimensions may seem intimidating. Rest assured, the former is only a matter of perspective, the latter easily overcome by working from two different rolls. The lesson to be learned is give yourself an opportunity to live with a pattern before committing to it. This extra step may save you from a costly and exasperating mistake.

Preparing to Hang

If you are tempted to hang wallcoverings yourself, do it! As with any project, having the right tools and being properly prepared goes a long way toward keeping a challenging process an enjoyable experience.

Avoid the nightmare of a project started late in the day. Deciding that seven at night is not too late to start hanging a wallcovering can lead to frustration and an unfinished project at midnight. Being tired always seems to create more difficulties than tackling a project fresh and well rested. The best do-it-yourself sequence is to plan the project, strip the old paper, and prepare the wall surface one day, and hang the new wallcovering the next.

Initial planning involves examining a room to determine the least conspicuous spot for starting and stopping, because it is unlikely that the pattern is going to match exactly at that point. A good spot may be a corner, or over the least-noticed doorway where there is only a small amount of paper. Another method is to determine where the focal point of the room is and start there, work to the start/stop point, then return to the first (focal) strip and continue in the other direction. This works well when it is important to center the pattern, particularly when hanging large patterns. In a room with a natural focal point, such as a fireplace, it is important to have a prominent piece of the pattern centered exactly over the mantel.

Although rare, mistakes in the pattern do occur. Wallcovering companies advise inspecting each roll for any imperfections, usually in the print registration. If found, the companies are generally very amenable about exchanging them.

STRIPPING WALLPAPER WITH PUTTY KNIFE

USING A LONG LEVEL

STRIPPING is a major part of the task. If the existing paper is not readily strippable or peel-able, spray the paper with a commercial wallcovering stripper solution, which is faster and cleaner than the homemade recipe of white vinegar and warm water. A small, round serrated scoring tool that creates superficial tracks is a help; it encourages the solution to penetrate. Use a putty knife to get under a loosened piece and, with a large trash can at the ready, tug, pull, or scrape away the old paper, immediately disposing of it so you will not have to pick the sticky pieces off the bottom of your shoes. After stripping, wash the wall with water and vinegar to remove any residual paste. To give trim a fresh appearance, paint it after stripping off the old paper but before applying the new wallcovering.

PREPARING the surface of the wall promotes professional-looking results. Spackle holes left from picture hanging and any dents or imperfections in the wallboard, and lightly sand the entire wall when dry. With new construction, walls must be primed before hanging wallpaper. It is also helpful to size the wall; sizing is a product applied to primed wallboard that dries quickly and provides some "slippage" when positioning the paper. It also speeds up the process of removing the paper when ready to redecorate, because it restricts the absorption of paste into the porous wallboard. Older walls, cracked plaster, and less-than-perfect surfaces benefit from a layer of liner paper as a substrate wallpaper. Liner paper is a plain paper that simply smoothes the surface of the walls.

A FINAL TASK before hanging paper is to establish plumb lines. A plumb line is a straight vertical line used as a reference for aligning the edge of the paper. This can be done with a plumb bob and chalk line, or a long level. It is not advisable to use the edge of the ceiling as your reference point as ceilings are often not truly straight. Plumb lines need to be established at the start point and a couple of inches away from each of the corners in the room.

Hanging the Paper

At last, it is time to hang your new wallcovering. With a drop pattern, when several rolls of paper are needed, plan to work from two rolls—Roll A and Roll B—concurrently. This is a professional trick that is a well-kept secret; the results are perfection.

- Cut your first strip from Roll A and hang it. Line up the next strip from Roll B; expect the first cut on Roll B to produce perhaps as much as 2 feet (0.6 meters) of waste (depending on the amount of drop). From that point on, however, where the cut on Roll A leaves off, that pattern is picked right up by Roll B.

- Another trick of the trade deals with solid color or random match patterns. The color from left to right is likely to differ very slightly; when it is hung, this variation becomes noticeable. Every other strip should be hung top to bottom, with the intervening strips reversed, "top" down and "bottom" up. This will keep like edges aligned with like edges. A subtle herringbone pattern with a slight color shift, when hung without this top-to-bottom matching method, can be very noticeable.

- For a room with an 8-foot (2.4-meter) ceiling, cut a strip about 8' 4" (2.6 meters) long. Loosely rolled, place it in a water-filled trough for the amount of time the manufacturer has recommended. Pull it out gently, unrolling it as you do so, and fold it over onto itself, glue side to glue side, to "book" for a couple of minutes. This booking process activates the paste.

- Using a small stepladder, attach the paper at the top, aligning the edge along an established plumb line. Use a wallcovering tool called a wide brush to smooth out the paper. Work from the center up and then from the center down, smoothing out the air bubbles. There may be an occasion to lift some of the paper and reposition it if it doesn't line up properly or if there is a stubborn bubble. Although some instructions call for piercing air bubbles with

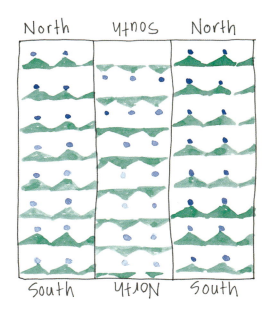

HERRINGBONE PATTERN PAPER
NORTH TO SOUTH—SOUTH TO NORTH

BOOKING THE PAPER

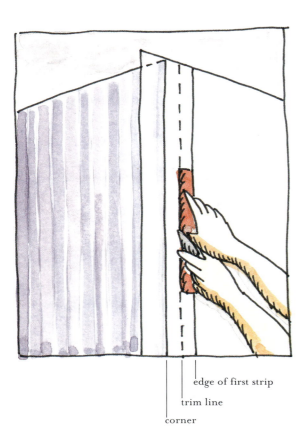

edge of first strip

trim line

corner

DOUBLE CUTTING METHOD

a knife or pin, it is best not to abuse the paper in that way. Use a straightedge in the form of a broadknife to hold the paper at the ceiling or floor molding, and a sharp utility or craft knife along its edge to cut away the extraneous inch or two of paper. It is imperative to always have a razor-sharp cutting tool; anything less will "chew" at the wet paper. A utility or craft knife with a series of snap-off blades is ideal. Break off a new point every two strips.

- Plan the next strip to line up perfectly with the previous strip. Again, with a random match or a small print with a short repeat, this is easy. If the drop match is considerable, resort to the Roll A/Roll B process. It is advisable not to continue wrapping the paper around a corner to any extent. In other words, when you approach an inside or outside corner, plan to cut your strip vertically so that it only wraps past the corner by an inch or two. When you hang the adjoining strip, the edge will probably not be the factory-cut edge. There's a professional technique called "double cutting" that makes the transition in this case nearly flawless.

- Match the next strip of paper, overlapping it by a couple of inches, and with a fresh blade on your knife, use a long straight edge (a metal yardstick is ideal) to trim from top to bottom through both strips. Lift the edge of the top strip to remove the excess of the bottom strip. Reposition the top strip. It will align perfectly.

- Throughout the project, after each strip has been hung, wipe the seam with a weak solution of soapy water to remove any excess paste that might have squeezed out. If left, it will discolor.

- Finally, glance at each wall from an angle. If you see any shiny spots, give them one last wipe to remove any paste you may have missed.

- It is advisable to keep leftover paper in case it gets damaged. If needed, a patch can be made by removing a small area around the damage and replacing it with the exact cut of the pattern.

Challenging Situations

Papering a room can be simple. Unfortunately, not all rooms allow for such simplicity.

- Bathrooms fall into the not-so-simple category. Because of their fixtures, tile, and installed cabinets, there are obstacles that create a challenge to cut around. Where there's a protrusion such as a bathroom tissue holder, adhere the strip and score the paper over the holder by making an X, allowing the fixture to punch through.

- Carefully cut away most of the unneeded paper. Smooth the strip on the wall and around the area. Trim along the edge of the fixture as you would along the ceiling, using the broadknife and a razor- sharp blade. Light fixtures and exhaust fans can be handled the same way. You may need to make overlapping Xs with these larger protrusions. Electrical switches and outlets are treated in the same fashion but require less exactness because a switch plate will cover the cuts.

- Windows and doors offer another challenge. As with fixtures, there is a relatively easy solution. Allow the paper to fall over the frame. Cut away excess, leaving about an inch and a half to be trimmed. Cut a diagonal or miter at the corner, which will allow you to "ease" the paper into place. Trim right up to the frame.

- With more complicated cuts, such as around windowsills where the apron molding is more detailed, take your time and cut around one contour at a time. Rather than use a utility knife on these difficult cuts, use a fingernail to score or crease the outline of the contour on the paper, lift the strip slightly, and trim with cuticle scissors.

TISSUE HOLDER POKING THROUGH
X CUT IN PAPER

TRIMMING AROUND TOP OF
DOOR/WINDOW FRAME

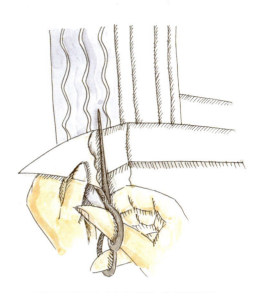

TRIMMING AROUND BOTTOM
OF WINDOWSILL

- When the room is finished, go through scraps of leftover paper to cover electrical outlet covers and switch plates to create a professional finish. Line up the pattern, then cut out a piece slightly larger than the cover. A little *X* needs to be cut where the switch comes through or the holes for an electrical plug are located and its pieces folded back to the other side. Tape can be used to secure these pieces, if it seems the glue's adhesion is not strong enough. With a sharp point, punch the paper where the screws fit through.

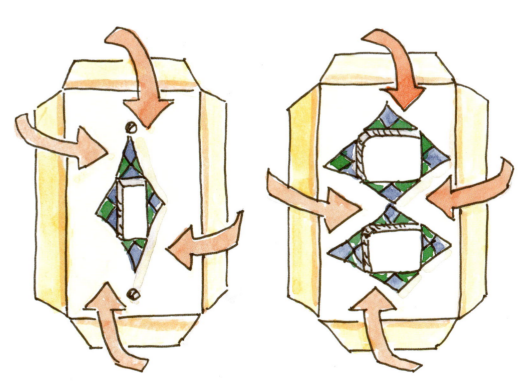

BACK OF SWITCH PLATE AND BACK OF OUTLET COVER

Printing Practices

Whether for borders or wallcoverings, the printing process is interesting in itself. There are four major wallcovering printing processes.

•

SURFACE PRINTING is the same as block printing but in its automated form; a brass roller is etched to produce the design. As a mental illustration, imagine a rose motif. To create definition, the brass between the petals is cut away, as is the area surrounding the flower head. Also cut away is the area around the stem. The veins in the leaf on the stem are etched out to add more realism. The resulting stemmed rose is inked each time the roller is rotated. This roller stamps the pattern on the paper as it is web-fed through the printer.

Surface printing is still the favored process of high-end wallcoverings. The image tends to be a little less exact than with other printing methods, which appeals to those desiring an original look to the motif.

•

Fine mesh screens are used in the *SCREEN PRINTING* process to block out areas not intended to be inked. Employing virtually the same methods used to silkscreen T shirts, the ink is applied to the paper in only the designated area. Using the rose again as an example, the mesh area surrounding the rose is sealed so inks will not penetrate, while the design of the rose on the mesh is left open to allow ink to seep through.

Screen printing allows for more colors to be used than surface printing. After drying, a printed area can be re-inked to create a stronger color or a shadow effect.

•

FLEXOGRAPHIC PRINTING is quite similar to the surface printing method, but the roller in this case is softer, almost like rubber. Thus, the inks in the design are more evenly spread and don't typically carry the effect a hard roller leaves. This process uses less ink, which means finer details can be realized and the paper dries faster.

Decorator stores will be glad to show you the difference between a surface-printed pattern and a flexographic-printed piece. It is likely you will favor one over the other.

•

GRAVURE PROCESS is described as the reverse of both the surface and flexographic processes in that the design is recessed, as opposed to being raised. The pockets of the design on the roller hold the inks. This allows for tonal hues and a virtually unlimited color range. The newer images, which look almost like a painting, take advantage of this process.

Selecting Wallcovering for Every Room of the House

THE LIVING ROOM offers space for a highly personal interpretation—what does "living" mean to you? Do you do a lot of entertaining? Does the music of a piano resonate within this space? Or is it the most active room in the house, a place to watch the evening news, groom the dog, remind the children to do their homework? Irrespective of its daily use, the living room is a place where families gather for special occasions, and the combined aspects of familiarity and formality coexist here.

Living rooms often enjoy the benefit of large windows. Where views are dramatic, a subtle pattern on the walls and ceiling will not steal the show. For gardeners, a floral pattern complements the blossoming landscaping during the growing season and makes up for the lack of it during dormant months. In traditional living rooms, a foulard print creates a nice backdrop. If a living room functions as a family room, a small geometric print can lead a double life, like the classic little black dress that can be dressed up or down. This is a room most likely to benefit from the use of design-matched fabrics; a chair or two upholstered in a fabric that matches the wallcovering can be stunning. In a large living room, a medallion or border perimeter treatment on the ceiling further enlivens the room.

THE KITCHEN is often referred to as the heart of the home. It is here where our daily nourishment is stored, stirred, and served. It is also a room in which a great deal of activity occurs. For this reason, a good scrubbable-type wallcovering should be selected, whether for the ceiling or the walls.

Many wallpaper patterns designed for the kitchen are as richly detailed as a still life. Apples look realistic enough to bite into. Steam seems to rise from loaves of freshly baked bread. Collections of plates look dimensional, owing to trompe l'oeil shadows behind them. Typically, kitchen motifs are small to medium in size, scaled to account for their use between upper and

lower cabinets and in and around appliances, without losing definition. And a gingham or check pattern never looks inappropriate in a kitchen.

A large kitchen ceiling benefits from a pattern that coordinates with that chosen for the walls, while a small Pullman-type kitchen looks larger when the ceiling is papered with the same pattern to create a seamless appearance. For those who prefer painted walls in a kitchen, a dramatic touch can be added by papering its ceiling only.

THE DINING ROOM is a place in which to enjoy good food, fine drink, and stimulating conversation. For that reason, the room naturally leans toward more formality than an eat-in kitchen—a great chance to use large patterns and dramatic colors. Because a chair rail makes sense in a dining room, this is an opportunity to use coordinated patterns above and below the rail. In dining rooms with high ceilings, the intent may be to enjoy the spacious feeling of height but with a welcoming coziness that encourages lingering conversation. By papering the ceiling, this effect can be achieved—the room still feels large, but the overall pattern makes it feel warm and intimate.

THE BEDROOM is a sanctuary, a place to which we retreat: to sleep after the excitement of a wonderful day, to find solace from sadness, to lay in the arms of the person we love, to recover from illness. A room in which we spend a third of our life. Why not paper walls and ceiling in a way that reflects how special the bedroom is? Surround yourself with a pattern that suits and soothes, regardless of your emotional state—one that is not too busy, not too bold, but not too bashful. When covering the ceiling of the bedroom, look for something you can literally stare at for hours. Fact or fiction, it is reported that Oscar Wilde's dying words were "Either this wallpaper has to go or I do."

THE BATHROOM is the room most likely to get papered and repapered frequently. For practical reasons, bathroom walls benefit from the moisture barrier that wallcoverings provide. Papers designed specifically for the bathroom are usually vinyl, although resilient, normal wear and some steam-loosened seams are bound to occur. The average homeowner is likely to replace the bathroom paper every seven years.

Contemporary homes usually contain more than one bathroom, often in space allocated within the interior of the floor plan. As a result, many bathrooms and powder rooms are windowless, and a light, reflective overall color of wallcovering is a good choice; though a powder room can also be papered in dark, rich colors that reinforce a precious feeling.

The powder room (or "half bath"), which doesn't suffer from steam and is most often used by guests, is likely to be papered with an exquisite, expensive pattern—as if this room were a little jewel box. It is an ideal place to use rich, hand-blocked, custom prints (often made available only to the trade) on walls and ceiling.

Ceilings of bathrooms, in which the user intends to enjoy long soaks in the tub, can be enhanced by papering. Much like the bedroom, choose something you really enjoy looking at.

THE DEN OR LIBRARY is usually an informal, functional room. For that reason, wallcoverings that suggest a relaxed and cozy ambience—plaids, deeper colors, faux wood, woven grass—are a timeless choice and make a good backdrop for framed diplomas, certificates of achievement, and collections of family photos.

Flooring

Flooring Predates Houses

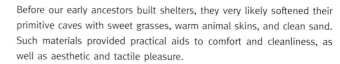

Before our early ancestors built shelters, they very likely softened their primitive caves with sweet grasses, warm animal skins, and clean sand. Such materials provided practical aids to comfort and cleanliness, as well as aesthetic and tactile pleasure.

Flooring still performs the same functions. As far as we've come in the vast world of house construction and design, we still want our floors to feel good and look great. If, in addition, they dampen sound, smell good, reflect light, age beautifully, or make it easier to keep the room clean, all the better.

That's the beauty of flooring: One of the most basic and functional components of a house provides an astonishing variety of decorative choices. There are few materials that someone hasn't tried to put on a floor at some point; some as unexpected as glass, metal, bamboo, or leather are surprisingly successful in the modern home. The familiar standbys such as wood and ceramic tile have benefited from techno-logical improvements that make them easier to install and maintain, more affordable, and available in a greater variety. If you think you know flooring, look again; advances in manufacturing processes and in the development of bonding and finishing materials have made some of the most familiar old flooring brand new. A common complaint in the hous-ing world is: "They don't make it like they used to." In flooring, the opposite is true: Before now, they didn't even make a lot of what is available to us today.

Whether you are building a new house, adding to your present home, or refurbishing a room, emulate those ancestral cave dwellers. In other words, install flooring for comfort, cleanliness, and aesthetic and tactile pleasure. Don't be afraid to indulge your cravings for luxury or beauty or progressive design. The floor, as the largest horizontal surface in a room, is vitally important to a unified design scheme. One definition of "floor" is "a surface as a foundation." When you think about the elements of function, comfort, and beauty that are so important in your home, think flooring. The foundation of a room is a logical place to start when you are developing an overall design scheme.

After all, you can't have rooms without floors, so have the flooring you want. So much is available, at so many price points, that it's easy to feel overwhelmed. Use this book to help guide your decision-making process. Take advantage of the information we've compiled about the variety of choices in today's marketplace while relying on your own likes, dislikes, and functional requirements. If you learn all you can while trusting your own instincts and taste, the result is bound to be flooring that works well, looks good, and is uniquely suited to you and your home.

Working Out a
Game Plan

Think for a moment about fashion. Imagine the most spectacular, glamorous ensemble that you can conjure up. Now, finish that outfit off with a pair of dowdy or simply inappropriate shoes. That's how important picking out the right floor is to finish—indeed, even to serve as the foundation for—a beautifully designed room.

Just as a pair of shoes can make or break an outfit, the right floor is integral to holding together the design and décor of any space. No matter how attractive a room, or how carefully chosen its furnishings, it will not shine unless the floor—or floor covering—is as breathtaking as the space that surrounds it. And just as fashion designers are continually creating, re-creating, and reinventing footwear for the shoe-obsessed, home designers are continually introducing new materials, styles, and colors of flooring, and in doing so, are reinventing home design.

Imagine a bathroom decked in dark pieces of slate, accented with sparkling glass, or a kitchen outfitted with thick planks of solid cherry. These might be a far cry from the tile or linoleum that typically cover these spaces, but remember, you don't have to be conventional to have a floor that works in a room. A floor is about more than having something to walk on. It's about understanding and working with different materials and deciding what they convey to you and to anyone who enters your home. New flooring is about building style in a room, from the ground up. ■■■

New and classic: the beauty of wood in an ecofriendly look-alike.

Use laminates for color and high-traffic areas.

Consider the Options

While natural hardwoods, stunning tiles, and luxurious carpets are among the most popular options, old-fashioned treatments such as classic linoleum and rich, supple leather are resurfacing in both modern and renovated homes. New alternatives, including laminate flooring and custom-tinted concrete, merge style with practicality to stunning effect. And a bevy of new flooring materials derived from renewable—even recycled—materials offers ecofriendly and uniquely beautiful alternatives to old-fashioned floors.

Streamline your choice by remembering that your floor is about more than appearance. Consider the way a floor plays to most of your senses: sight (the color, look, and light-reflecting qualities); sound (how it affects the room's acoustics); touch (cold or warm underfoot, hard or soft); and even scent (the subtle aromas of leather and linoleum, the way rugs can trap odors). Think not only about the style of the room but the practical requirements: A high-traffic vestibule requires something durable, while a cozy family room benefits from the warmth and sound-absorbing qualities of wall-to-wall carpeting.

New Floor/Old House

Installing new flooring in your old house is an opportunity to introduce style that's fresh, new, and tailored to today's lifestyle, while taking advantage of the quality construction that is the hallmark of many old houses. When you explore the options in today's flooring world, you may learn to see your old house in a new way. New flooring can serve to highlight the character and charm that first attracted you to your house.

Highlight What Works; Help for What Doesn't

Small, cramped rooms, for example, can be visually enlarged with beige wall-to-wall carpeting. Choose a beige with yellow undertones to bring warmth into the décor; if you want a cool effect, choose a gray beige. If you would like to emphasize the warm tones in old woodwork, lay carpets or install resilient flooring in saturated reds and greens that bring out the colors of mahogany or oak. Rooms in your old house may have good proportions that have gotten lost in fussy or unfocused decorative schemes; here is a chance to show off their "good bones." Stencil or paint the floor in geometric or border patterns, install pale stone tiles, or lay one of the new neutral-colored sisal carpets that are bound with a contrasting cotton border. Chose a size and shape that follows the outline of the room, leaving a 1- or 2-foot (.3- or .6-meter) perimeter of bare floor. The border color can echo wall or upholstery colors or it can strike a dramatic note in a neutral room.

Use new flooring to emphasize what's best in a room, whether built-ins, a wonderful view, beautiful woodwork, or good furniture. A superb collection of antique furniture can be showcased to great effect against a backdrop of cutting-edge flooring. Imagine the impact of gilded Louis XVI chairs on a floor of glass tiles or a curvaceous Rococo Revival parlor suite with red plush upholstery arranged on flat gray wool wall-to-wall carpet. One effective way of calling attention to a particular piece is to place an area rug under it; one well-known example is the style icon of a rocking chair on a braided rug. A jewel-toned prayer rug could serve as a frame for a glass and steel coffee table. Put your leather and rosewood Eames recliner and ottoman on a deep shaggy rug in white or cream. Emphasize the pure lines of a Shaker table by placing it on dark gray slate. In each instance, the impact of each piece is heightened by the choice of flooring or floor covering.

Consider Your Old Floors a Plus

Chances are good that they are structurally sound; well-built floors can be the basis for a new look without great expense. A common scenario for the new owners of an old house is to rip up worn-out resilient flooring, only to find a crude, unfinished wood surface that requires some sort of covering. Consider some of today's decorative paint products, which can provide surprising texture and color. For instance, you might apply two contrasting colors of supremely tough paint, then "comb."

Historically, it was not unusual to install new hardwood over an existing softwood floor; in this case, the old floor became part of the subfloor. Many of today's flooring options (vinyl sheet or tiles and "floating" floors, to name only two) can be installed over existing flooring. Use manufacturers' guidelines when you lay one material over another. Cork floors, for instance, should not be installed over linoleum, vinyl, or rubber since the materials experience such different rates of expansion and contraction. Once you've ascertained the compatability of the different materials, the primary thing to keep in mind is the thickness added by each new layer. Doors should swing without touching the floor; baseboards and wall elements should not be compromised. Also, remember the overall proportions of your room. A mere inch can make the difference between pleasing proportions and an awkward fit in some rooms. Since many of today's laminates, vinyl floor tiles, and resilient sheet-flooring varieties are newly slender, many more options are at your disposal than in the past. Even ceramic tile and stone flooring are thinner today.

Historic character and charm are highlighted with a new wood laminate floor in a dark chestnut color. These modern floors can "float" over the surface of existing flooring.

When to Start Over

When should you go through the (not inconsiderable) effort of ripping up existing flooring? Keep in mind that all flooring problems do not mandate a new floor: Rough, stained, discolored, blemished, burned, or gouged wood floors can usually be cured by refinishing. Squeaks, probably at the top of the list of reasons why people want new floors, can be isolated and silenced. Even more serious old-floor problems are fixable. A wood floor may have been sanded and refinished too many times, causing planks or strips to break down, especially along the edges. Deep scratches or dents may mar the surface and present safety hazards. Old resilient flooring may have worn through to the subfloor or underlayment; tiles may be cracked, grout deteriorating. As distressing as these problems are, repairs can usually be made. Experts on the subject of old houses advise that most old floors stand a greater chance of remaining stable if they are not disturbed. If you are not sure whether you should work with what you have, contact a qualified house inspector. He or she can assess the structural soundness of your floors and can often counsel you in the best ways to address problems.

Paint is one of the most effective and least costly ways to refresh the appearance of an old floor. For a less traditional effect, consider faux finishes or trompe l'oeil.

STILL THE SQUEAKS AND CREAKS

IN MOST CASES, A CREAKING FLOOR IS CAUSED BY
LOOSENING OF THE NAILS HOLDING THE SUBFLOOR TO
THE JOISTS. IF THE CREAK IS IN AN EXPOSED SUB-
FLOOR, AS IN A BASEMENT, DRIVE A SMALL WEDGE
BETWEEN THE JOIST AND THE LOOSE BOARD ABOVE IT.
IF IT IS IMPOSSIBLE TO REACH THE SUBFLOOR, LOCATE
THE JOIST BY TAPPING ON THE FLOOR, THEN DRIVE 2-
OR 3-INCH (5 OR 8 CM) FINISHING NAILS THROUGH THE
FLOOR, SUBFLOOR, AND INTO THE JOIST. USE A NAIL
SET TO DRIVE THE NAIL BELOW THE SURFACE OF THE
WOOD SO THAT YOU DON'T HIT THE FINISHED FLOOR
WITH THE HAMMER AND MAR THE FINISH. THEN FILL
THE HOLE WITH PUTTY OR STAIN THAT MATCHES THE
FLOOR.

IF A LOOSE BOARD IS THE CAUSE, YOU CAN LOCATE THE
BOARD BY ITS MOVEMENT WHEN WEIGHT IS PUT ON IT.
USE 2-INCH (5 CM) FINISHING NAILS, DRIVEN AT AN
ANGLE, TO FASTEN IT. THEN USE THE NAIL SET.

*A new kitchen in an old house
called for a compatible floor; in
this case, honey-toned knotty pine
echoes the rustic old post-and-
beam construction.*

Troubleshooting: Framing and Structure

There are deeper, hidden reasons for floor troubles, and sometimes an old floor is simply
beyond help. Perhaps your house had a persistent leak: If water worked its way in and caused
rot, then the floor will have to be replaced. Defective framing can cause sagging and sloping
floors. Floor joists that are too small or inadequately supported can also be the reason for
uneven floor wear. (If this is the case in a house you are considering for purchase, keep in
mind the truism that poor carpentry in one area is a tip-off to substandard construction
throughout the house.) Floors that have been exposed to water may warp or bulge upwards.
Wide cracks between floorboards are a sign of poor workmanship or of shrinkage caused by
wood that was improperly dried or not stored correctly at the time of installation. Or perhaps
the subfloor suffered damage, in which case, the whole section must be replaced to the
nearest joist.

New structural beams can be "sistered" to the old. In this process, failing old weight-bear-
ing elements are not removed but rather attached to strong new ones. If space does not allow
this, new steel beams or columns provide optimum strength.

If you do install a new floor in an old house, choose what harmonizes with the interior's
overall design scheme. If the house is architecturally important, extremely old, or a great
example of a specific decorative style, you will probably choose to reproduce the original
flooring. In most cases, however, the options are only limited by your taste and budget.

Starting Fresh
Build in Your Choices from the Start

Few things are more thrilling than planning a new home of your own. This is the opportunity to define your preferences and to act on them, thus creating a living space that is uniquely yours. Flooring is a crucial element in beautiful décor: Think floors when you first consider your home's style. Include your flooring choices in the plan from the beginning to avoid costly and disruptive changes later on and create a decorative scheme that is a stylistic whole.

Some flooring can be laid directly over a cement slab. Terrazzo, ceramic tile, and concrete are a few examples that require no additional subflooring between those materials and even incorporate cement in the installation process. Whatever the material of your subfloor, now is the time to work out issues of compatibility. In new construction, your only concern is apt to be the differential rates of expansion and contraction between the subfloor and the finish flooring. With forethought, these concerns can be minimized or even eliminated.

Advance planning will determine color schemes and assure that materials are ordered in sufficient quantities. If, for instance, your floors are intended to tone from lighter to darker as you walk deeper into your house, this is the time to assure that it will happen just the way you want—long before unmatched flooring meets an expensive construction crew.

Think about all your flooring issues and you'll be ahead of the game. You'll want to give primary consideration to your likes and dislikes, but don't stop at aesthetics. Think about whether you like the work of maintenance associated with some types of flooring or whether you are the no-muss, no-fuss type. How important is noise? Does your definition of luxury include sinking into deep pile with every step? And then there's longevity: Are you willing to pay more for a floor that will last longer? Some kinds of flooring show the dirt more readily than others; professionals must install some. Does anyone in the home have needs that mandate particular features? Examples might be nonslip walking surfaces for elderly or visually-impaired family members or easy-to-clean floors in a household populated by children and pets.

A carefully planned work alcove under the stairs gains design coherence from a neutral floor that continues up the stair treads.

Start with Style

Start with a clear sense of the house's style. Whether it is formal, casual, traditional, modern, country, or urban will dictate its design vocabulary, including the flooring. Decide what you want the flooring to do, other than to provide a surface to walk on. This might include dampening sound, calling attention to a particular area, providing a backdrop for a collection of rugs, or showcasing a beautiful local material such as wood or stone.

Is a compatible combination of bright colors your personal bliss? White walls and simple design make way for color exploding up from the floor.

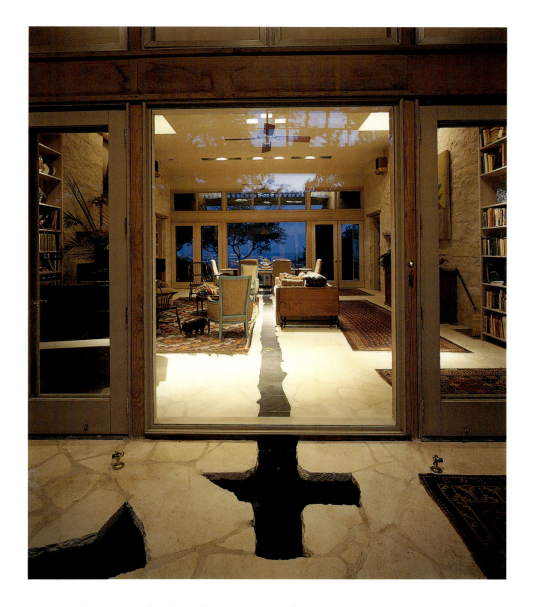

You may wish to play up the drama of a broad expanse of space or create intimate conversation areas. If you include flooring in your design plans, rooms will come together more gracefully.

This is a great time for list making. Write down what matters to you, what you need, what you want—and enjoy!

Timing is Everything

Some kinds of flooring, concrete and stone among them (above), are most easily installed while the house is under construction. Pouring and curing concrete, hauling heavy stone, troweling, clomping about in caked work boots—these are not done comfortably near finished surfaces. It's also better for your health to avoid heavy-construction sites (and to take appropriate protective measures, such as wearing masks and respirators, when doing it yourself). Other types of flooring, such as hardwood, should not be laid until the room is further along in structure and finish. Laminate floors can even be laid in a room that's more or less furnished. Leather flooring requires a week's acclimation, during which time you can't use the room. So, think ahead and plan your new floor construction for your own comfort and convenience.

The Floor and
Design Implications

Deciding on the right floor for a particular room is not about taste alone. You have to consider the size and shape of the room, its architecture, furnishings, style, the amount and quality of natural light, and the room's purpose. Once all these elements have been carefully weighed, you can consider the different materials that might work in a room, and the way each of your options can provide a multitude of different results.

When you begin your flooring process, plan (for new construction) or determine (if already established) a room's overall use, appearance, and personality.

This quality is sometimes hard to pinpoint, since personality (in homes as well as in people) comes together from so many intangible and subtle elements. If your home is a strong example of a specific architectural style, or a combination of styles, your decorating efforts will be easiest and most successful if you know what it is and follow its directions. You may choose a design scheme that is not customary for the house's architecture, just as you might dress in a surprisingly unconventional way, but if this is done without knowledge and intent, the result is rarely flattering.

Architecture and Flooring: A Marriage of Style

Architecture provides the style definition. Look to the moldings, window openings, baseboards, mantelpieces, and other architectural elements (or lack thereof) to determine whether the space is formal, classical, modern, or rustic. In older houses, especially, these will mirror the house's exterior style elements. General characteristics can be further narrowed down to a definition of the house's individual style. This is often a reflection of the popular tastes of the time at which the house was built. Often (though certainly not always) a shortcut to determining house style is to know the date of construction, and then to match it to interior and exterior design elements. But if you can't exactly pinpoint your home's age or style, don't worry. Many older houses were added to over time, thus changing or diluting their original stylistic statements. In recent decades, houses were often built with design elements borrowed from a number of sources, pared down, or reinvented.

A stylish flooring personality may be hard to define, but it is unmistakable when seen. Here, materials are mixed in surprising ways for effective and practical traffic flow.

As you study the details that make up your house's stylistic whole, you will come to recognize it as formal or informal, plain or highly ornamented, casual, urban, minimalist, romantic, country, or eclectic. In other words, you will get to know your house's design statement, even if that can't be pigeonholed into one recognizable style definition.

The Right Floor for the Room

Once you have determined your house's style and whether you will create a stylistic whole or 'work against type,' your first question is use. Form really does follow function, and your room will work best if you install the floor that is best for its intended use. An obvious example of this is the fact that vinyl, stone, or ceramic tiles, not inlaid wood or antique Oriental rugs, are popular in bathrooms.

The first experience of a floor is tactile. Your mind registers a soft rug, hard marble, or creaky wood, and your initial preference will be biased for a floor that is hard or soft. The

Dare to work against type—a sisal carpet instead of the traditional pine boards or hooked rugs emphasized the furniture in a country bedroom while suffusing the whole scheme with calm and warmth.

room's use, of course, will help you make this determination. Visual cues can effectively under-score this message. The flooring surface establishes the primary horizontal plane in a room and underlies the entire design scheme you want to communicate. Gray wall-to-wall carpeting, for instance, unifies space, whereas scattered Oriental rugs establish distinct walking and seating patterns, as do stenciling, inlay, borders, or center medallions. Give some thought to the subtle messages communicated by materials: Leather floor tiles hint at the atmosphere of libraries or of comfortable retreats; bamboo speaks of the Far East; dark gray slate evokes the severe beauty of northern winters.

Think about the effects of reflected light. Very shiny floors look cold; matte flooring gives the appearance of softness. The way light plays off the grain or wood or the surface striations in stone is part of their beauty; use these materials to highlight these characteristics.

Mood is set by color. Brown may be the color that comes to mind when you think of a wood floor, but it is just the beginning of a range of colorful possibilities. Likewise, ceramic tile is often laid in a monochromatic earth-toned or checkerboard two-tone scheme, but tiles are so colorful that you can have a rainbow on your floor today. In fact, you are not limited to conventional effects, as most kinds of flooring are now available in great color ranges.

Style is personality. Underlying a furniture arrangement of simple elegance and saturated color is classic, unadorned flooring.

Take advantage of the choices for mood-altering design impact. Light-colored floors will make a room appear larger, while dark floors promote an intimate atmosphere. Texture, too, contributes to the mood; a smooth, unbroken surface feels streamlined. A mixture of materials gives the impression of depth and complexity. Natural materials in earth tones can appear to bring the outdoors in. For a modern look, use pale neutral floor colors to give the room a clean, uncluttered appearance.

Color and Pattern

If your floor is tiled, carpeted, stenciled, or painted, choose an overall pattern that is consistent with the room's other decorative elements in color, formality, architectural style, and drama. The size of a pattern is important, but scale is even more important. Generally, small patterns work best in small rooms, and large patterns in large rooms—but don't underestimate the dramatic possibilities of large patterns in small rooms. Just make sure that the scale of the pattern is consistent with your overall design statement. For example, in a small room with hefty architectural elements such as boldly scaled moldings or a massive overmantel, scale the floor patterns to those elements, not to the size of the room. Keep the rest of the décor simple to achieve this successfully; otherwise, you are apt to create visually claustrophobic clutter. A small, modern room grows when pale, neutral-colored furnishings rest against a bold, overscaled pattern on the floor.

Use carpeting to create a pattern. Lay area rugs to lead the eye toward a focal point or a distant view.

Pattern can be a thorny issue in today's interior designs. Use what works for you, and if you keep your home's innate personality in mind, you won't go wrong.

A pale wood floor, painted and stenciled, forms the base for the dreamy, tranquil aesthetic of a seaside home. Flooring colors, carefully matched in the décor, echo the outdoors.

Furniture placement determines how we move through a room. Flooring is the best way to establish sections of specific use, whether with area rugs, or by laying flooring in pathways and seating areas. For example, place a carpet under the dining room table or outline the area under it with a different color of the same material. To correct a difficult-to-follow layout, continue the tiles from the entry to the living room threshold, or toward the stairs. Your kitchen floor might be surfaced in hard-wearing vinyl tile, with a breakfast nook or seating area defined with a different color tile or outlined with a border. Moving from hard to soft flooring is an excellent way to signal use areas; for example, when the wood floor of a hallway is broken with an area rug under a telephone table and chair.

Dark flooring, here in stained concrete, promotes intimacy, something used to great effect in a colorful, lighthearted breakfast nook.

New Shortcuts to Flooring Personality

Aluminum, stainless steel, and zinc floors speak of a sophisticated, urban aesthetic. Decorators often use this hard-edged statement to punctuate other flooring, especially in spacious lofts. Metal flooring can be particularly effective when used to define traffic paths, use areas, and staircases in vast, open spaces or to evoke the atmosphere of a Soho loft in an otherwise traditional building. Another cutting-edge look increasingly found in today's architecturally designed interiors is that of stained concrete. Both metal and concrete can be softened without compromise to their industrial look with area carpets that have an exaggerated depth of pile in the new paper, natural fiber, or synthetic designs. Computer-printed carpeting in high-tech-derived images sends an unmistakably modern message. Or, to create an avant-garde atmosphere steeped in subtlety, think of sisal or flat-woven worsted wool carpeting installed wall-to-wall in shades of taupe or mushroom.

Modern Looks

Other materials appropriate to sleek, luxurious modernism are polished stone, rubber, neutral wall-to-wall carpeting, or a sophisticated vinyl. For the unmistakable look of the Moderne period, use cork flooring in rectangular patterns, perhaps with a border or use terrazzo in

period-appropriate designs and colors. Update the look by choosing tertiary colors in vogue today—warm taupes, grayed blacks and whites, yellowed greens, smoky blues and purples, and dusty pinks and peaches.

Sleek, luxurious modernism is expressed in highly polished stone. Shades of black and gray provide pattern and sophistication.

Classic Looks

Thin stone and wood parquet flooring tiles, backed with easy-to-install mesh, are the modern shortcut to refined, classic interiors rich with moldings, silk draperies, antique furniture, and fine art. In these types of rooms, areas are defined with Aubusson rugs or Persian carpets.

Country Looks

At the folksy end of the design spectrum is the Southwestern or Spanish Colonial room, with its massive ceiling beams and rough plaster walls. Here, terra-cotta Mexican tile or honed stone pavers are an important part of establishing a well-loved rural design personality. Heighten the level of interest of this look with wood: Wood laminates and engineered flooring allow the use of mixed materials without the expensive and time-consuming custom work required in the past.

A country farmhouse interior is best evoked with wide pine boards, complete with knots and other surface imperfections. Fortunately, you can get this look without having to spend a few generations achieving it; you can find it in today's engineered floors, in reused old flooring, and in laminates. Wood floors can be painted, stenciled, bleached, or left untreated and scattered with hooked, braided, or woven area rugs. Flooring, like the rest of the house, is unpretentious, simple, and colorful. Another charming flooring choice for this kind of décor is linoleum, especially in the retro colors and patterns that recall kitchens of the first part of the twentieth century.

Arts and Crafts homes feature flooring that seeks to bring nature indoors and to echo the house's natural surroundings. Local wood or stone, accented with tribal rugs, underscores the handcrafted elements of these homes. Achieve this atmosphere with a recently introduced hardwood flooring type, in which richly colored and patterned oak varieties are bonded together into wide pieces of uniform length. Finger-joining, as this is called, is also available in engineered flooring and it creates a handmade flooring look with unprecedented ease of installation.

Bamboo flooring creates subtle patterns and echoes similar hues in the sand of a faraway beach.

A CYBER STROLL THROUGH THE WORLD OF FLOORING

HOW DO YOU SEE VAST REALMS OF FLOORING WITHOUT SPENDING YEARS ON YOUR FEET? YOU PROBABLY ALREADY LOOK AT PICTURES IN BOOKS AND MAGAZINES. NOW GET ON-LINE: AN EVER-INCREASING NUMBER OF MANUFACTURERS POST THEIR PRODUCTS ON THE INTERNET. THE BEST SITES FEATURE LUSH PHOTOGRAPHY, DETAILED SPECIFICATIONS, ANSWERS TO FREQUENTLY ASKED QUESTIONS, AND INSTALLATION TIPS. GO THERE, AS WELL, FOR INFORMATION FROM TRADE ORGANIZATIONS, ON-LINE RETAIL STORES, AND THE OFTEN-INVALUABLE INPUT FROM OTHER CONSUMERS. ELECTRONIC BROWSING CAN LEAD YOU TO THE BEST FLOORING STORES AND FLOORING DEPARTMENTS OF HOME-DESIGN STORES AND TO PRODUCTS YOU MAY NOT HAVE KNOWN ABOUT. THEN, WHEN YOU ACTUALLY STRIKE OUT TO SEE, FEEL, SMELL, AND TOUCH THE FLOORING THAT INTERESTS YOU, YOUR SEARCH WILL BE FAR MORE STREAMLINED AND PURPOSEFUL, AND FAR MORE REWARDING.

Floor
Issues

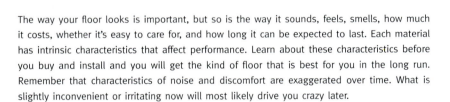

The way your floor looks is important, but so is the way it sounds, feels, smells, how much it costs, whether it's easy to care for, and how long it can be expected to last. Each material has intrinsic characteristics that affect performance. Learn about these characteristics before you buy and install and you will get the kind of floor that is best for you in the long run. Remember that characteristics of noise and discomfort are exaggerated over time. What is slightly inconvenient or irritating now will most likely drive you crazy later.

To ascertain your own personal flooring issues, make a list of general qualities and characteristics of a home that are important to you. You may never have associated some of these with flooring, but write them down anyway. You probably know whether you find dark rooms depressing; be aware that some kinds of flooring absorb (instead of reflect) light. Some people value tactile qualities above others, some have great sensitivity to sound. Whatever consistently pleases or displeases you should go on your list. For some, it is very important that the materials in their home come from nature. There are people for whom the way a thing or place looks is always the most important aspect; for others, aesthetics are always secondary to cost considerations. If you hate dirt, write it down. This is the place to list aversions and positive associations. Perhaps you have unhappy memories of a particular kind of floor; you won't want to inadvertently re-create it in your home. Does cork remind you of the 1950s décor of your favorite aunt? Write it down. Maybe the smell of linoleum recalls a happy childhood. Your list is uniquely your own and it will help you to remember what you want if the flooring sales staff is giving you the hard sell. ■ ■ ■

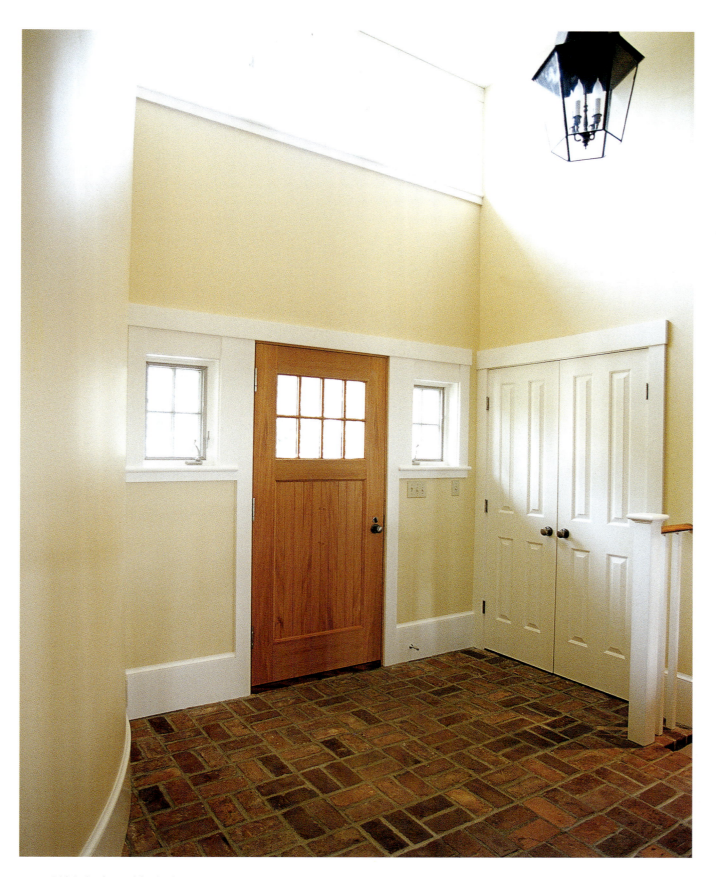

Brick is time-honored flooring in an entry. Brick is not dirt-sensitive, will absorb and hold solar heat from the windows above, and it signals informality and transition from the outside.

Aesthetics

No matter how "perfect" a particular type of flooring material may be for its intended use, if you don't like it, it's not right for you. You may feel pressured by considerations of cost, practicality, historic precedent, or momentary fashion, but you are the one who will live with the flooring installed in your home. Choose what appeals to you. There are so many flooring options available today that you should not have to settle for anything you don't want to see every day. Even if one material is presented to you as "the only thing that will do," there is usually at least one acceptable substitute. Today's superb cutting, milling, and bonding technologies have created new permutations in almost all flooring materials. They can be made to look or act like something entirely different from what they started out as, with little or no compromise in quality. Know what you are working with in terms of architectural style, intended use, personality, and price range. Then, follow your heart.

Cost

The cost of a floor is often greater than simply the cost of the material. In a showroom, the per-square-foot cost given for each type of flooring does not include the cost of labor. Depending on the installation process, this can be a little or a whole lot.

An example is the great range of prices associated with the various types of wood floors. Laminate wood flooring is appropriate for do-it-yourselfers and is manufactured to resemble a number of wood species. It can be installed with no labor cost except for your own time. Except for a possible foam underlayment, it may not require any additional tools or materials. Laminate flooring can be priced quite reasonably. Solid hardwood flooring is at the other end of the cost spectrum. Oak, maple, and beech are expensive, and installing the strips or planks is time-consuming and demands a level of skill and equipment that often requires professional installation. Depending on the subfloor, a vapor barrier or wood sleepers (wood members embedded in concrete that serve to support and to fasten subflooring to the floor) may be necessary. And, unless the hardwood strips are factory-finished, sanding and sealing the floor add to the expense. Engineered floors fall somewhere between these two extremes. They can cost as much as solid hardwood, but do-it-yourself homeowners can often install them.

When ascertaining the cost of any type of flooring, take into consideration the material cost, labor costs, costs of related materials, tools or equipment, and the amount of time installation will require. Make sure to ask whether any materials need to be acclimated to their site before or after installation. While this may not add to the installation cost itself, you do need to know whether you'll be able to use the new room right away, or whether the finish on your bedroom floor dictates a couple of nights at a hotel.

Solid hardwood flooring is the gold standard for deeply traditional interiors. It is beautiful but expensive.

- If you use colors the way they appear in nature, then the darker colors should be on the lower portions of the room. Dark colors carry more visual weight.
- The best room color schemes should have a single dominant color.
- Colors appear darker and more intense in large areas than in small ones, particularly in spaces where light is reflected, strengthening the color vibrations.
- Color on aged surfaces usually displays a yellow component due to the yellowing of the finish.
- Wood and metal colors should be factored into color schemes.

Color

If you crave color underfoot, be grateful that you were born into our modern times. There are no more color taboos of taste or décor, and modern technological advances keep on producing familiar materials in unfamiliar shades and new materials in a huge array of colors. Given that anything is possible, here are a few general color rules (to be broken with good reason).

Make color part of your flooring design vocabulary. A red and white rubber floor, supremely practical, brings life to a laundry room.

Color	Effect on space	Effect on mood
Light colors, pale neutrals, bleached woods	enlarges space, makes space airy	quiet or tranquil
Medium-value nonintense colors, neutrals, fruitwood	diminishes space slightly	conservative
Deep colors, dark stained woods, black	diminishes space, erases boundaries, lowers ceilings	dramatic or traditional, old-fashioned
Autumn colors, Mahogany, rosewood	diminishes space substantially	cozy, rich, very warm
Pale blue or green	enlarges space	serene, suggests the sky
Dark blue or green	diminishes space	mysterious, suggests the sea, cool
Yellow	enlarges spaces	suggests sunshine in good lighting

What Goes with What

Classic	Simple use of rich materials, Oriental rugs, hardwood parquet
Colonial	Wide softwood boards, honed pavers, brick, stenciled or painted boards, floorcloths
Country	Knotty pine, linoleum, bleached, painted or stenciled, floorcloths, hooked or shirred rugs
Modern	Stone, cork, rubber, vinyl, hardwood, pale neutrals, unbroken expanse
Romantic	Stenciled, carpeted, rugs on carpets, softness
Victorian	Wall-to-wall floral or patterned carpets, linoleum, saturated colors

Classic

Colonial

Country

Modern

Romantic

Victorian

Flooring
Factors

Noise/Tactile

When it comes to the way floors sound and feel, remember that flooring materials are divided into "hard" and "soft." Soft flooring materials are the most resilient—cork, linoleum, vinyl, rubber, and carpeting. These are the quiet flooring materials: They dampen and absorb sound. Hard flooring includes ceramic tile, concrete, metal, stone, and, to a lesser degree, wood. These materials reflect sound. Generally speaking, the harder the material, the greater its sound-reflecting properties. Thus, wood flooring, which is softer than stone, ceramic tile, or concrete, is only marginally "hard." Even the hardest wood commonly used for flooring, which is maple, absorbs sound, though not as much as a resilient floor. Real wood feels softer than wood laminate flooring, which has the properties of hard flooring.

If a quiet floor is at the top of your list of design criteria, you have probably already considered carpets. But think about incorporating cork into your flooring plans. Cork's ability to deaden sound has long made it a favorite in recording studios, hospitals, concert halls, libraries, offices, and gyms. It is the flooring material you wish for your upstairs neighbors if you live in a noisy apartment building.

A floor composed of cork tiles is expensive, but beautiful and comfortable. If solid cork is beyond your reach, or if you don't care for the look, be aware that cork is at the core of some engineered flooring, lending sound-absorption to their properties. ■ ■ ■

Noise is an important flooring issue to consider. Stone floors reflect and magnify sound.

Cleaning and Maintenance

Even the lowest-maintenance flooring gets dirty. Floors are at the bottom of the room, and gravity being what it is, that means dust settles on them, things fall down onto them—and then there's the stuff on all those feet (and paws) that walk all over them! A floor that's heavily traveled will get very dirty—period. And, as your mother might have told you (had you been paying attention), if the floor looks clean, the room looks clean. Keep this in mind when making flooring choices. Regardless of how much you like the look of ceramic tile, it is not the right flooring material for you if you hate to wash floors. If you are allergic to dust, steer clear of deep-pile carpets because you will never be able to vacuum them enough to keep dust out of the fibers. There is no flooring material that is completely maintenance free, regardless of what sales people may try to tell you.

Left: Not least among flooring issues is that of cleaning. Do you like a floor that always looks immaculate? White is a good choice for this look; just remember that lots of maintenance keeps it looking fresh.

Above: A tile floor is a time-honored kitchen favorite. It requires daily sweeping to keep the tile surfaces from getting scratched.

How to navigate through the universe of
flooring choices available—from glass to
metal, leather to paper, wood to stone—
and find the one that's perfect for you.

Flooring Solutions: New and Classic

Flooring Solutions:
New and Classic

There isn't a building material you can't put on your floor, if you have the inclination, the budget, and the right place for it. Glass? Sure—brilliantly colored glass tiles can punctuate other materials, or even shine on their own. Leather? Absolutely—this deeply natural flooring now comes in delicious designer colors. Paper? Oh, yes—it's being woven into fabulously fanciful textured rugs. Porcelain? Sure—it's very hard, and has a way with color. Metal? It's very cool—steel floors have been moving out of factories and onto the floors of the avant-garde. Plastic? Now *there's* a modern building material! It goes on and on.

Whenever a new material is invented, designers rush to find applications for it, and that includes walking on it. Of course, most flooring materials have been around for a long time, periodically rediscovered by a new generation of homeowners and decorators. That's part of the beauty of the world of flooring: It can be traditional to the point of becoming boring, until a creative designer uses a familiar material in a new way. The ways different materials are put together keep on changing, and as bonding technology gets better and better, new combinations keep popping up.

Working with Wood Laminates

The most popular floor sold in the Western world today is the wood laminate floor. No wonder: It's a brilliant use of modern materials yet traditional in its appeal to the average homeowner. Laminate flooring is versatile, affordable, can be installed by unskilled do-it-yourselfers, and it can go where wood floors can't—onto another floor, below grade, into an old house. These floors are self-contained systems that are almost unaffected by structural limitations.

Their composition comes from a chemical lab, not a forest. Layers of composite materials are compressed under high heat and sandwiched around a core that might be made of wood products or, at the product's high end, cork. Most often, the bottom consists of a paper product that acts as a vapor barrier. The floor elements come in thin (some measure as little as 1/3 inch (.84 cm) thick) tongue-and-groove planks, just like hardwood flooring, but are not nailed to the underfloor. Instead, these floors "float" on the surface. Glue holds the planks together to form a one-piece floor. At their best, wood laminate floors have a high tolerance for spills because there are no open seams where water can go. Because they are not nailed to a subfloor or to floor joists, they are not apt to develop squeaks, but they do tend to sound hollow. They do not offer the comfort of wood flooring since they are harder.

The term "wood laminate" is already a bit of a misnomer. The early wood laminates resembled hardwood, and this is still the best-selling format. Photographed wood grain finishes the top, making a high-tech product look like a traditional wood floor. But laminate floors today are made to resemble stone as well as complex wood patterns such as herringbone, parquet tile, and contrasting checkerboard weaves. Since all these designs are photographs (of parquet or of stone), there is no limit to the possible appearance of a laminate floor. The surface characteristics of the material it resembles are embossed or molded into the wear layer; ever-better photo printing technology provides the visuals, and the result is pure alchemy.

Be aware that the characteristic shine of laminate tends to be visible at the edges of recesses in the material: there are connoisseurs who claim that they can always recognize a laminate floor. But twentieth century advances in vinyls and laminates have been so progressive that generalizations are nearly impossible. Use them instead of stone, ceramic tile, cork, rubber, or linoleum if you want those looks for less. Digital technology doesn't stop with hard flooring materials. The latest carpet technology applies computer know-how by using sophisticated dye-injection processes to print digital images onto the surface of the fibers. Patterns take details from the modern world, from satellite images to interactive Web sites, as reference. This is an unapologetically high-tech floor covering for twenty-first-century homes.

Stained concrete has achieved new levels of sophistication and aesthetics. Today's staining or etching products can achieve results that combine the traditional appeal of stone with seamless modernism. The easiest to use are applied to cured concrete with sprayers such as super-sized plant misters or insect sprayers. To date, about half a dozen colors are available, with more coming onto the market all the time.

Top Left: The world of flooring no longer breaks down into "hardwood taste, softwood budget."

Top Middle: Metal is one of the new flooring materials currently favored by architects and designers in lofts and other modern interiors. Sensible handrails provide safety and security with these metal stairs.

Top Right: The well-loved wood laminate floor brings together the best of modern technology, traditional good looks, and ease of installation.

Colorful Laminates

Stained Concrete

Latex-backed Woven Paper

Left: Yesterday, wood laminate was considered the cutting edge in flooring. Today, the technology replicates other materials; in this version it could be called "stone laminate."

Right: Stained concrete is supremely modern: It can be colored and waxed to match any décor; it is tough, and an integral part of the structure.

Stone

Ancient and venerable, stone is nevertheless a sophisticated modern flooring material. From a design perspective, stone is at its best after years of use, unlike other materials, which are best new. In twelfth-century European cathedrals, we walk on flagstones and stair treads that have been gently shaped by thousands of feet over hundreds of years. The stone is worn, but far from worn out. What the years of use have done is to add immeasurably to the floor's beauty. Stone is the rare thing that actually improves with age. Continued use bestows a mellow patina, so that even the simplest of stone floors eventually achieves a luxurious dignity. Stone flooring is associated with security, permanence, and solidity, and for good reason—it lasts virtually forever.

Stone is less cumbersome to install than you might think; modern cutting technology produces stone flooring tiles that measure a slender $1/4$ inch (.5 cm). (As with any floor, however, do confirm that the subflooring is sound.) Elaborate center medallions and decorative borders, once the exclusive purview of the wealthy, are now available as separate components in home centers and building supply stores. At the sumptuous end of the spectrum, 48-inch by 24-inch (122 cm by 61 cm) slabs can be custom-fitted to a room, resulting in a sleek floor with the unparalleled visual impact created by the stone's natural markings flowing over a large unbroken surface. Designers also achieve beautiful results with recycled old stone—roofing slates become flooring tiles; limestone flags from demolished French farmhouses see new life in American kitchens.

marble

limestone

granite

Known Stone

When you install stone flooring, you will want to incorporate its natural beauty into the room's overall design scheme. Stone differs from cement and tile, the other hard flooring materials, in that it is not manufactured. From a design standpoint, stone has more in common with hardwood; it is a natural product whose decorative features of color and pattern are intrinsic.

The varieties of stone most commonly used for flooring are:

■ Marble
■ Limestone
■ Slate
■ Granite

Limestone, slate, and marble in natural, honed, or aged finishes (without a high shine) are stylistically suited to rustic, Arts and Crafts (Mission), or Moderne (Mid-Century Modern) house styles.

Polished marble in colors ranging all the way from black to white is a traditional favorite in formal entries, galleries, and high-style traditional rooms. Today it is also the flooring material of choice for lavish spa baths.

The amber, cream, taupe, and gray tones of limestone, combined with its porous surface texture, make it a favorite in farmhouse kitchens. Limestone slabs with pronounced patterning are design favorites for dramatic living rooms.

Slate is extremely dense, does not burn or stain, and has a distinctive flake. Long used for hearths, it is also a bathroom favorite. Slate is newly popular in kitchens and in rooms designed to bring in the ambiance of the out-of-doors.

Because stone is so durable, it is well suited to entry halls, stairs, kitchens, bathrooms, and other high-traffic areas. The luxurious aspect of stone flooring makes it an ever more popular choice for living rooms, where area rugs are the logical choice to soften walking surfaces and dull sound. The shiniest types of stone flooring—polished marbles and granites—are also the slipperiest, so a reliable nonskid pad under rugs is important from a safety standpoint.

Stone is a cold material, a fact that once made stone floors traditional in dairies. If you are considering a stone floor, think about installing underfloor heating. Modern stone floors are easily installed over radiant electric or hot-water heating systems, and, once warm, the stone's mass holds the heat for a long time.

Stone is expensive—despite better quarrying, cutting, and installation technologies, a stone floor still costs more than its ceramic tile counterpart. However, the cost of the stone floor is quite reasonable when the price is amortized over its long life. This longevity makes stone inadvisable in stylistically dated patterns, unless the homeowner wants a time capsule underfoot.

Left: Because it is so durable, stone can be recycled and adaptively resued. This earth-toned kitchen floor was once a slate roof.

Middle: Stone floors can be highly polished and formal or rough and rustic. What they have in common is the fact that their beauty transcends the moment, getting bettter with time.

Right: Polished marble flooring is formal, dramatic, and makes a strong design statement in a small entry hall.

The characteristic good looks of dark gray or black slate are practical as well as handsome in a bathroom.

TERRAZZO PIZZAZZ

TERRAZZO IS OFTEN PRESENTED AS AN ANCIENT STONE PRODUCT AND, WHILE IT IS STONE, IT IS ACTUALLY A TWENTIETH-CENTURY BUILDING MATERIAL DESCENDED FROM THE ART OF MOSAIC AND ORIGINALLY KNOWN AS CONCRETE MOSAIC. MARBLE CHIPS MIXED WITH COLORED PORTLAND CEMENT FORM A MATRIX THAT IS POURED OVER A CONCRETE BASE AND STABILIZED BY MEANS OF METAL DIVIDER STRIPS. ONCE CURED, IT IS GROUND AND POLISHED TO A SMOOTH FINISH OR, LESS OFTEN, LEFT IN A RUSTICATED STATE.

TODAY'S TERRAZZO IS THINNER, MAKING IT MORE USEFUL FOR HOMES. BEAUTIFUL AND STRONG, THIS IS A GOOD CHOICE FOR THOSE WHO WANT STONE FLOORING WITH A MORE TECHNOLOGICAL LOOK OR A PATTERN COMPLEXITY THAT'S EITHER UNAVAILABLE OR PROHIBITIVELY COSTLY IN SOLID STONE. BECAUSE OF ITS METHOD OF CONSTRUCTION, TERRAZZO IS WELL SUITED TO THE SMOOTH, CURVY DESIGNS OF THE ART DECO AND MODERNE STYLES, WHICH ARE CURRENTLY SEEING A STRONG REVIVAL IN INTERIOR-DESIGN SCHEMES.

SOME OF THE MOST INTERESTING TERRAZZO FLOORS USE THE METAL DIVIDER STRIPS AS PART OF THE DESIGN STATEMENT. MOST OFTEN BRASS, THEY CAN BE COPPER, NICKEL, SILVER, ZINC, STEEL, OR ANY OTHER METAL WHOSE COLORS FORM A THIN CONTRASTING OR COMPLEMENTARY BORDER BETWEEN FIELD COLORS. THE MATERIAL IS NOT LIMITED TO MARBLE MIXTURES, EITHER. ONYX, TRAVERTINE, SERPENTINE, EVEN GLASS, CAN CREATE TERRAZZO PIZZAZZ.

Terrazzo is not new technology, but in homes it always looks fresh and surprising.

Wood

Wood — Classic and Cutting Edge

Few materials can withstand the test of time quite the way that wood does. A natural wood floor gives a room unmistakable warmth, reflects natural light, and fits in seamlessly with almost any décor. And a good-quality wood floor can last a century or more—just take a look at some of the beautiful, turn-of-the-century wood floors in landmark homes today.

But choosing a wood floor is not as simple as calling a contractor and ordering one. You have to consider the type of wood, the application, and the color and finish—and each decision you make will affect the overall look of the room. Solid wood floors do have some limitations. They are not the best choice for areas that tend to get wet because wood expands and contracts when exposed to dampness. Installation itself poses some problems, too. Most wood floors must be nailed into place, making them poor choices for basements and other rooms constructed on concrete slabs. And newly installed wood floors might come up as much as 3/4 inch (2 cm) from where the previous floor was, creating a troublesome and potentially hazardous little step up from one room to another.

Luckily, modern manufacturers have offered solutions that make wood floors more accessible. Floating laminate floors in simulated wood grain can be installed in basements and kitchen without worry and can float easily over concrete subfloors.

Wood is for warmth: its hues, texture, and sound quality play to the senses.

Engineered wood flooring combines the best of wood and high-tech materials. A distant descendant of plywood, an engineered wood plank has a top wear layer of solid wood applied to alternating layers of other wood materials. Because the layers are perpendicular to each other, there is great strength in this type of wood flooring. An advantage of engineered wood flooring is the fact that, unlike solid wood, it can be installed as "floating flooring."

Finger joining offers another alternative to the way hardwood has traditionally been sold: in strips 2 $^1/_4$" (7 cm) wide and $^3/_4$" (2 cm) thick. Finger-joined boards are composed of small end-matched pieces bonded together, resulting in wide 7-foot (2.1 m) pieces. Environmentalists like finger-joined hardwood flooring because the smaller pieces of wood are a more efficient use of natural resources. And, the uniform lengths result in shorter installation times and thus, lower overall cost.

Factory-applied finishes are a great boon to homeowners; as soon as the wood floor has been installed, it can be used. Factory finishes are uniform and applied under dust-free, temperature-controlled conditions for optimal curing. Polyurethane, when exposed to ultraviolet light, cures almost instantly. Now urethane factory finishes are routinely uv-light cured. Even newer is the use of ceramic or aluminum oxides in the finish. Although the amounts are too small and the particles too fine to be visible, ceramic or aluminum oxides mixed with polyurethane make for an extremely tough surface layer.

If you simply must have real wood, consider parquet flooring—made of smaller pieces of wood glued into tiles that can be glued into place—which can add real-wood character to rooms where nails won't work.

If you're looking for something as beautiful as wood and as tough as stone, acrylic-impregnated wood flooring—natural wood pressure treated with a tough-as-nails acrylic finish that goes right through the entire plank—is yet another option. With the color and finish penetrating every pore of the wood, these floors are highly resistant to scratches, scuffs, and moisture, and so can boldly go where few wood floors have gone before—the mudroom, entryway, kitchen, and beyond. Available in the same styles as wood laminate, acrylic-impregnated floors are often used in commercial spaces where foot traffic (including wet, muddy feet) is high and have recently become available to residential customers as well.

Style, Substance, and Pattern

Once you've decided on wood, you need to think about the style and substance of your floor. Think not only about the wood itself but also the installation. For example, if your room is long and somewhat narrow, a straight installation of thin hardwood planks will be your best bet—the repeated lines make the room look wider. You can add a high-gloss finish that reflects natural light to further the illusion of space. Even the sound quality of the wood floor, a warm yet definite echo, suggests a room of larger dimensions.

Planked horizontal installations of wood can make long narrow rooms look subtly wider.

A Palette in Wood

Oak with oil finish

Red Oak

Unstained Oak

Planked Birch

Mahogany

Knotty Pine

Cardamom Stain

Saffron Stain

Cobalt Stain

A large, open room makes an ideal setting for experimenting with pattern. A herringbone pattern creates interest on the floor while at the same time making the room appear less vacuous. And a room that is defined by architectural details—a stunning hearth, built-in bookcases, or floor-to-ceiling French doors—benefits from inlaid borders that draw the eye out toward the perimeter of the room.

Put similar thought into your choice of wood. A high-traffic kitchen might demand a tough hardwood like oak or maple, while less-traveled bedrooms could work just as well with soft, warm knotty pine. Think about the grain and overall look of the wood, and consider how it fits in with your personal style. Are you going for a modern, streamlined look? The heavy grain of oak or walnut might not work as well in your ultra-modern loft space, but thin planks of clear beech might be just your style.

And what about color? Once installed, a floor can be finished in an endless variety of tones—ash, for example, while beautiful in its natural state, takes on an entirely different character when stained a deep cherry, and achieves another look altogether when tinted colonial blue.

Matching your floor to your furnishing is important, but perhaps less important than one might think. While the style of the floor should complement the décor and dimensions of the room, matching the floor precisely to the furnishings might be a mistake. For example, gorgeous Georgian furniture of deep, dark cherry is lost when matched with a floor of the same wood, stain, and finish. But a floor of bright, unstained natural oak or maple, with a semi gloss finish and trimmed out with matching floor molding, creates a stunning but subtle backdrop, while the furniture plays a starring role.

Wood floors also offer flexibility. They make beautiful backdrops for antique or unique area rugs, which can be used to warm up rooms during cold winter months, and removed to reveal a cooler-looking and airier space in the heat of summer. This option allows a homeowner to dramatically change the look and feel of a room without making major renovations.

Tile

When you install a tile floor, you have the opportunity to create something personal and unique while following in the footsteps of countless generations of homeowners before you. The Egyptians invented fired-clay tile six thousand years ago; successive civilizations have never tired of reinventing the basic formula. Universal and familiar, the humble clay tile is often taken for granted, yet it is so versatile that its design possibilities are virtually limitless. And, in recent years, tiles have gone high-tech. Now there are aluminum tiles with a baked-enamel finish, steel tiles, cement tiles with a terra-cotta surface, glass tiles, and plastic tiles.

Whatever their makeup, all tiles are really just thin surfacing units that can be used individually or as part of a whole. This gives them huge design potential, a fact that has always made tiles irresistible to artists. If you want a truly creative floor, whether of your own or someone else's design, tiles can provide it.

Designing with tile can broadcast a message with wit, style, and subtlety. Use tiles to express something ethnic, geographic, historic, or personal about you or your house. Make a sophisticated statement with a high-tech combination of glass and metal, or plastic and baked earth. Celebrate colors in your natural environment. You'll find countless choices represented in the variety offered for sale, which may be the downside of shopping for flooring tiles. The world of tiles is vast and seductive; you can easily get lost in the grout. A tile floor, perhaps more than any other kind, calls for forethought. That involves commonsense basics, such as measuring and drawing out a floor plan of the room to scale. But think as well about color, tone, mood, scale, complexity of pattern, and range of colors. A striking design can become meaningless in a flooring footprint interspersed with furniture, wall cutouts, bays, and islands. Too-small or predictable patterns can look timid and frumpy. Borders can make a room look cluttered if not designed to echo the architecture, or at least fool us into thinking that it does. Colors that are scrumptious in 12-inch (30 cm) swatches can become a problem in an overall design. ■ ■ ■

At the same time, tile is a supremely practical flooring material with a long history in kitchens, bathrooms, entry halls, and other hard-wearing places that tend to get wet. The price range is nearly as vast as the selection, and tile floors can be laid by do-it-yourselfers (though elaborate installations are best done by those with some experience). One of the easiest kinds of tile to install is called ceramic mosaic. Smaller than than common tile, it is manufactured in sheets held together by a mesh backing. The backing offers correct spacing for the grout, which is applied later.

Tile flooring is one of the best ways to create a rustic design scheme full of irregular, patinated surfaces and earth tones. The familiar quarry tile is an ever-popular choice. Until recently it was only available in terra-cotta red, but now runs the gamut of earth tones from the palest sand to the darkest umber. Tiles are just as helpful for those drawn to the other end of the style spectrum—one route to a clean, hard-edged design is to lay a floor of precisely cut, smooth ceramic tile. Tile is created equally in the artisan's shop and in the automated factory; the smooth, mass-produced product is not considered better than the earthy handmade one. Each is perfectly suited to its intended use.

Ceramic tile, more than any other flooring material, is associated with colorful, ethnic design statements.

Guide to Glaze

Glazed tiles are made in various sizes and shapes and most lend themselves to floors. But high-gloss tiles should be used cautiously, both because of the danger of slipping and because a mirror glaze is easily scratched by grit carried into houses on shoes. One glaze that's been developed for tiles is known as a crystal glaze; it has a rough, granular texture, which is more or less slip-proof. Crystal-glazed tiles are among the most popular for floors.

Unglazed ceramic tile is a strong favorite for contemporary flooring. Part of its appeal is its association with warmth. Much beautiful unglazed floor tile comes from Mexico, and few things hold heat better than dark-colored, unglazed quarry tiles (hence their long history in solariums and greenhouses). But they are creeping into the rest of the house, especially in the desert Southwest, Florida, and California. From a design standpoint, unglazed quarry tiles or pavers can be used in any room of the house, except for the most formally decorated ones.

Tile's other design personality is sleek, modern, and monochromatic. Tiles are supremely versatile, both in materials and manufacturing processes and in their uses.

A Palette in Tile

Unglazed Stone Tile

Metallic Glazed

Wheel Thrown Tile

Crackle Glaze Tile

Glazed Clay Tile

Handpainted Tile

Iridescent Glass Tile

Terra-cotta Tile

Floral Tile

About Grout

Grout, the material that fills the joints between tiles, can make the floor more interesting. For graphic impact, chose a grout color that contrasts sharply with the tile. For a monochromatic, quiet effect, chose grout the same color as the tile. The grout is, in fact, an integral element when considering a tile floor, not as glamorous, but important to the design, expense, ease of maintenance, and long-term wear.

Also, tile is unforgiving of uneven subfloors. Specialists say that a 4-inch (10 cm) layer of perfectly smooth, level material must support a tile floor. If your floor flexes or has hills and valleys, then this is not the flooring for you.

Cork and Rubber

Fifty years after enjoying status as the flooring material of choice for style-conscious home-owners, cork is back. Actually, it is more accurate to say that the same cork that was such an important element in mid-century modern design is still very much in use. What is more, it was in use long before minimalist designers discovered its superb qualities as a building material. Cork was among the earliest resilient flooring products, and it has never completely gone out of style.

It's no wonder. Cork has resilience, natural good looks, and superb sound-deadening properties. It appeals to environmentalists because harvesting cork does not kill the cork oak tree. Grown primarily in Portugal and Spain, these trees can be stripped of their outer layer periodically, with no detrimental effect on the tree itself. A single tree yields cork over the span of 100 to 150 years.

Decorative Veneer Cork

A Palette in Cork

Scuff-proof

All varieties of resilient flooring, including cork and rubber, have a convenient ability to bounce back from scuffs and abrasions. Resilience, which also makes for comfort underfoot, comes in thin sheets and tiles. That means imperfections in your subflooring will show through, and may eventually lead to wear and deterioration. The importance of a good subfloor can't be overstated. It must be smooth, dry, and flat, and it must be free of dirt, grease, paint, or anything else that would hinder a good bond with the floor tiles' backing.

Marbled rubber floor tile is making a style comeback after years of absence. Its wonderful look is matched with toughness. Floors such as these are good for fifty years or more.

Carpet and Rugs

For homeowners craving a new look, a spot of color, a pattern to unify a room, or simply some fun and excitement in the décor, change is as close as a new rug. Imagine, for instance, the joy of a giant flower on your floor, its shape delineated by its great, curving, purple petals. New carpets aren't limited to squares, rectangles, circles, or ovals; their shapes can be very free-form indeed.

As for carpet color and design, the two newest trends aim for polar opposite effects. One applies pattern and color in the most high-tech way possible. Digital images are printed onto carpets via computerized dye-injection processes. Though any type of pattern is possible, early examples have featured images that draw on technology for inspiration, including satellite images and Web site graphics.

The other trend uses a modern dyeing process called tea staining to make brand new carpets look old. The term is a misnomer; no Earl Gray is actually used. For the gently aged look of an antique Oriental, modern dyes produce an overall amber cast that speak of elegant age but do not damage the carpet fibers in the process. Early efforts at weaving these shadings into the carpet proved unconvincing; tea staining is more successful at achieving this beloved look. ■ ■ ■

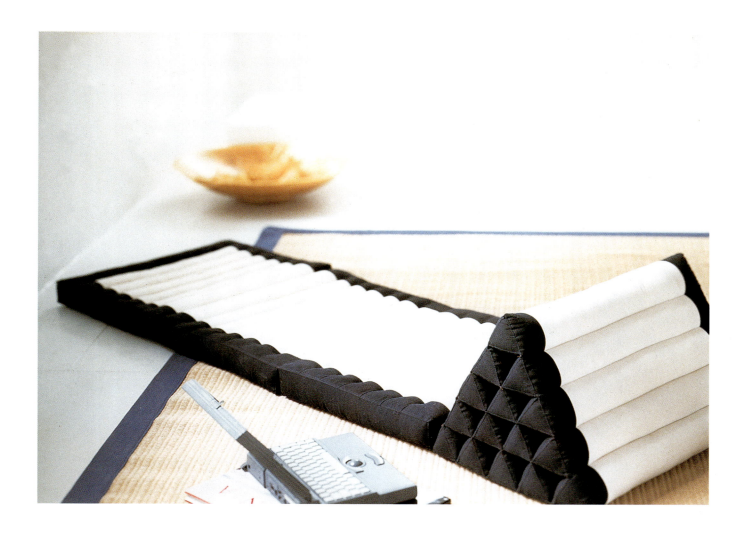

Beyond Traditional Wool

The best carpets are made of wool, woven either on a wool or cotton base, and the best carpet wool comes from New Zealand. Wool is strong, soft, and superbly dyeable. It is, however, expensive. Alternative fibers have been used since they were invented; some will provide the look for less but will not give the same consistent quality of wear. Recent favorites include sisal, coir, and seagrass. Seagrass is lovely, pale, and somewhat fragile, with the bonus of a faint but characteristic scent. Coir and, to a lesser degree, sisal, have a coarser texture than wool. Both have natural good looks in brown tones. Coir, especially, will rot if it gets wet; use coir carpeting only in areas not exposed to possible moisture.

The same is true of the new paper rugs, which make sly allusions to the look of wicker or the deep-shag carpeting fad of the 1950s. Their best use is in bedrooms, conversation corners, or other low-traffic areas.

Much modern carpeting can be custom-pieced for individual designs. You might, for instance, have stair carpeting climb up and down the steps in a color progression. Or you might choose contrasting or complementary colors for a carpet's body and border.

New paper-based materials let carpets mimic woven rush and tatami textures.

Enjoy the shaded tones of elegant antiquity in a new rug.

Floor Art for Sale

Carpets and rugs are brilliant examples of home furnishings as art. Utilitarian floor coverings are exemplars of local craft traditions all over the world. We take our carpets to heart in ways usually expressed among other flooring choices only by purists. People who love carpets love them a lot, and we see that reflected in everything associated with the world of rugs and carpeting. As with all forms of art, record prices are paid and misinformation abounds, so education pays off.

You can buy a piece of art for your floor without fear if you follow these guidelines:

- Buy from reputable dealers. An Oriental rug sold for an alleged 80 percent off during an oft-repeated going-out-of-business sale is likely not to be the rare beauty it's represented to be. Oriental carpet dealers with stable, customer-based businesses, on the other hand, can be vast and personable fonts of information on the subject. Many are delighted to educate potential customers and will happily answer questions. A reputable dealer will always tell you where your rug is from, what it is made of (wool, cotton, silk, and whether the dyes are vegetable or aniline), how it is made, and will let you take it home to try it out. Antiques dealers should be willing to take back a carpet and refund your money for any reason.

- Don't shop for art if what you really want is a red rug. There is such a wealth of choice available in the commercial carpet world that you may want to stop and consider whether you really want an antique hooked rug or the warm and colorful statement it makes. The antique is fragile and costly, and the current wave of appreciation for this appealing folk art form has spawned many companies that make new, practical versions.

- Please yourself. The best reason to put a piece of flooring art into your home is because you love it. With all the options that are out there, don't let yourself be pressured into buying what's chic, what's a good investment, what the most fashionable people you know say you should. You'll be looking at that carpet for a long time; make sure it will continue to bring you pleasure. That way, you'll still be happy even if the bottom drops out of the market for it, or if tastemakers change their minds about the design.

A Palette in Carpet

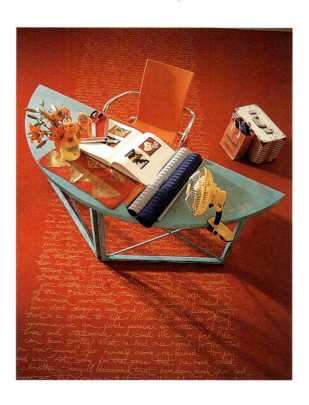

Flat Weave

Aubusson

Kilim

Needlepoint

Dashiki Pattern

Needlepoint

START WITH THE CARPET

A TRADITIONAL PIECE OF INTERIOR DESIGN WISDOM HOLDS THAT, FOR A ROOM'S COLOR SCHEME, YOU SHOULD TAKE YOUR CUES FROM YOUR CARPET. LIKE MANY OLD SAWS THAT HAVE BEEN REPEATED INTO MEANINGLESSNESS, IT STILL HOLDS A KERNEL OF TRUTH.

CHOOSE TWO OR, AT MOST, THREE COLORS FROM A ROOM-SIZED ORIENTAL RUG FOR THE ROOM'S FABRICS AND WALLS. HARMONY WILL RESULT, AND IT IS INFINITELY EASIER THAN IT IS TO TRY TO MATCH A CARPET TO ALREADY-EXIST-ING FURNITURE AND TEXTILES.

Glass and Porcelain

Of all the materials you might think to use to cover your floor, one of the more surprising, surely, is glass. To some of us it seems antithetical to walk on a substance so prone to shattering, one we associate with transparency, mirrors, and windows.

Great Looks in Glass

Yet glass is an extremely strong material that, when poured in thickness beyond what's required for windows, is nearly indestructible. Glass has an unsurpassed way with color, hardness that makes it a snap to keep clean, and comes in flooring formats that offer great value and design versatility. Glass flooring is impervious to frost, water, and stains, and highly resistant to chemical attack, fading, or discoloration.

A glass floor can be the ultimate statement about texture or color. It can be graphic, from modern to deco, or it can be sleek, neutral, and understated. It is always stunning. Remember that the single best feature of glass as a design tool is its ability to reflect, deepen, and echo color. Some glass tiles are fused, some poured into molds, and in some, the colors are painted onto the back. Each technique creates a different effect. An especially well-loved glass tile features the gentle, time-dulled surface of beach glass. The colors are powdery and soft but saturated as only glass colors can be.

As lavish and delicate as they look, these beautiful floors are cleaned with nothing more than a swipe of common glass cleaner. They should never be waxed but can be damp-mopped just like a tile floor.

CAUTION: SLIPPERY WHEN WET

THE LEADING CHARACTERISTIC OF GLASS AND
PORCELAIN—HARDNESS—ALSO PRESENTS A
SAFETY HAZARD. UNLESS YOUR GLASS OR
PORCELAIN FLOOR IS MADE WITH A TEXTURED
SURFACE, SMOOTHNESS IS APT TO BECOME
SLICK WHEN WET. INSTALL WITH SAFETY IN
MIND: PUT FLOOR-GRIPPING RUBBERIZED MATS
ON A BATHROOM FLOOR, KEEP GLITTERING
INSTALLATIONS OUT OF THE PATH OF FAST-
MOVING CHILDREN AND OF ADULTS UNSURE
OF THEIR FOOTING. NEVER PUT A SCATTER RUG
OVER GLASS OR PORCELAIN TILES WITHOUT AN
UNDERLAY DESIGNED TO STOP SKIDDING.
DON'T USE GLASS OR PORCELAIN FOR STAIR
TREADS.

*The clear colors of
glass and porcelain are
heightened by water and
work well in bathrooms.*

While you may not be ready for a roomful of glass underfoot, consider the design possibilities of setting glass tile into other materials. Here is an opportunity to add dimension to any floor; you might incorporate a subtly reflective border, pick out one color to accentuate or lend cohesion, or carry some design element into the floor in unexpected ways. Imagine the surprise of a thin line of cobalt blue or ruby red glittering in the quiet of an oak floor, or of an iridescent highlight in a floor of unglazed quarry tile.

One of the most exciting options available in flooring today is a glass mosaic rug resembling a classic Oriental or kilim. Small pieces of glass in all colors of the rainbow, from soft iridescent pastels to bold jewel tones, make up the carpet pattern, which can be set into nearly any kind of flooring. Designs are made to order and shipped on fiberglass mesh for easy installation with thin-set mortar and grout.

Porcelain Possibilities

In hardness, porcelain lies somewhere between glass and glazed ceramic. It is made from a white, nonporous clay that, when fired, has all the characteristics desired in fine tableware. Porcelain floor tiles are extremely hard and can be easily cleaned with glass cleaner, something that's not recommended for clay. Porcelain floor tiles do not provide the same richness and depth of color as glass but have equal resistance to staining, etching, and temperature fluctuations. They can be as versatile as clay tiles. Some porcelain floor tiles are as smooth as a dinner plate, while others resemble limestone.

Clear glass field tiles alternate with jewel-toned smaller tiles in a design whose brilliance belies its toughness.

A Palette
in Glass

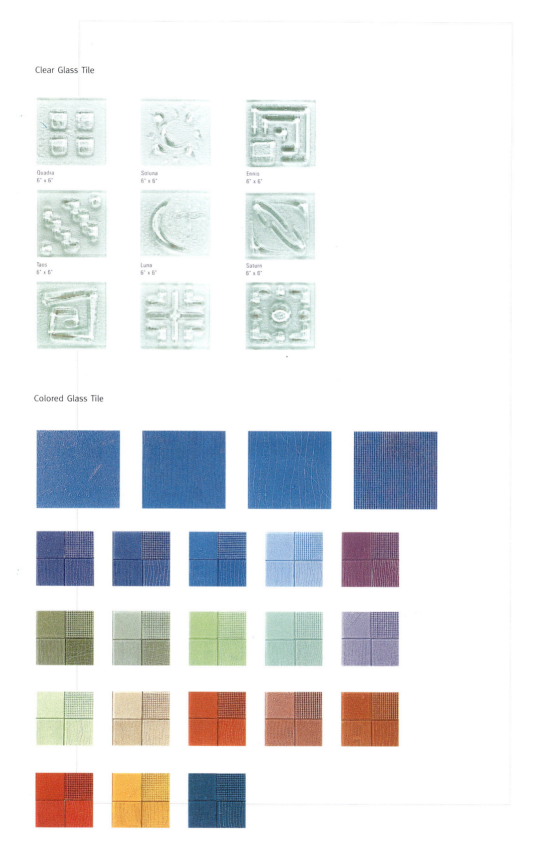

Clear Glass Tile

Quadra
6" x 6"

Soluna
6" x 6"

Ennis
6" x 6"

Taos
6" x 6"

Luna
6" x 6"

Saturn
6" x 6"

Colored Glass Tile

With a beautiful floor as a base, even a sparsely appointed room can look elegant and rich. Ordinary furniture takes on dignity, an almost-empty room can look glamorous and mysterious.

Designing with Flooring

Designing
with Flooring

Think of installing a new floor as a design opportunity; uninspired architecture can be lifted beyond the banal, less-than-pleasing proportions can be corrected. Because flooring has the ability to either fade into the background or dominate the room, its design potential is vast.

Use saturated color on the floor to bring a room's shape into focus or to correct the well-like claustrophobia of overly high ceilings in a small room. For an interesting jewel-box effect, try tinting the ceiling in a lighter version of the same color. A border can correct, or appear to correct, the shape of an awkward room; stencil, tile, paint, or use carpeting or resilient flooring to outline the shape of the room as you prefer to see it.

Especially if the design of a room or house is not to your liking, use flooring to create walking and seating areas. In an open layout, bold contrast leads the eye away from the parts you want to de-emphasize. If a house is chopped up into small rooms with little cohesion, use an overall pattern on the whole floor to unify space.

Instead of placing a carpet under the dining room table, where it will require constant cleaning and pose a possible safety hazard, define a rectangle around the table and chairs in a band of contrasting flooring. The greatest drama is achieved with a material different from that of the rest of the floor: wood timbers laid into stone, tiles set into wood, glass tiles into terra-cotta pavers. For a subtle and sophisticated effect, use different materials in similar colors.

To set off a kitchen cooking area or preparation island, outline it in flooring different from the rest of the room.

A small room can be made to look larger with a floor that's lighter than the walls. Keep in mind that every line of contrast constricts space; a pale expanse looks larger than one broken up with pattern.

If you want to bring the outdoors into a room, choose flooring that harmonizes with an element of nature seen from a window or door. This could include wood flooring in a species of tree growing outside, stone that echoes colors in the environment, or colors like that of a distant body of water. The most natural effects are achieved with materials that are not polished to a high sheen.

To play up the organic charm of an informal country kitchen, scatter small tiles in an irregular, seemingly random pattern onto a floor tiled with larger pavers. Do not space them too closely; if the room is large, use two different sizes of small tiles.

Large, alternating squares, whether in stone, resilient materials, or painted, give cohesion and a sense of design purpose to an irregularly shaped room. On the other hand, this traditional flooring approach can make a rectangular room look boxy.

Installed in a border long enough to repeat the pattern again and again, mosaic border designs can achieve a sense of movement and rhythm.

Top Left: Material and elevation can give a floor lots of impact; this light-filled sitting area becomes a special retreat, set off from the rest of the room.

Top Right: The colors and the rustic beauty of nature continue into an entrance hall paved with slate.

Bottom Right: Pattern, color, atmosphere, architecture—all can be created, altered, or emphasized by stenciling the floor. What's more, this is one craft that does not call for artistic expertise, just attention to detail.

Hardwood
and Softwood

Because it's been a favorite flooring material for so very long, wood's design potential has been explored in every imaginable way. Or so it seems, until contemporary flooring companies begin to produce wood flooring in new colors or combined with other materials in new ways or to bring a new wood variety into the mix. Sometimes they even (gasp!) use hardwoods and softwoods together.

Hardwoods versus Soft

The difference between hardwood and softwood is, obviously, one of degrees of hardness. In flooring, this translates into qualities of wear and cost. Hardwoods tend to be longer lasting, less vulnerable to scratches and nicks, and more expensive than softwood. But there is a place for softwood flooring in the modern home. Some of the softer woods, notably the pines, firs, and larches, are loved for their distinctive patterns and colors. Generally, softwood floorboards are available in wider widths than hardwoods. The look of a pine floor is a style icon: If you want this in your country kitchen, you have a practical option in extremely hard factory-applied finishes that incorporate suspended metal particles and are cured with ultraviolet light.

Wood floor strips and planks are usually laid perpendicular to the floor joists, but if the subfloor is sound, wood flooring can be laid diagonally. Another way of achieving design interest is with a herringbone pattern of narrow strips. Both the diagonal and the herringbone patterns can be useful in correcting unfortunate proportions. A too-narrow hall, for instance, can appear wider with a herringbone-patterned floor.

Some of the specialty finishes include bleaching, pickling, antiquing, and coloring. Strong caution is advised to do-it-yourselfers, however; these are best applied at the factory, since they can damage the wood and can cause personal injury and environmental damage.

A RADIANT FLOOR

The news about under-floor radiant heat is that it can now be installed under wood floors. Today's flooring professionals cite advances in manufacturing, such as finger-joining, which has recently brought this economical and practical heating technology to wood for utterly comfortable flooring. The systems are best suited to narrow-strip hardwood floors that experience minimal seasonal expansion and contraction; planks over 3 inches (8 cm) wide won't work. A network of hot-water-filled tubing runs under the floor, warming it and the room. The water in the system is continuously returned to the water heater for constant, even heat.

A QUICK GLOSSARY OF STAINS AND FINISHES

SPECIALTY FINISHES AND STAINS ARE WAYS TO EXPAND YOUR DESIGN OPTIONS WITH WOOD FLOORS. HERE'S A QUICK RUNDOWN:

STAINS DARKEN THE WOOD BUT PRESERVE THE APPEARANCE OF THE GRAIN. CLEAR FINISHES SHOWCASE THE NATURAL COLOR AND GRAIN. VARNISHES AND SHELLACS PROVIDE A HARD FINISH BUT ARE NOT WATERPROOF, WHILE URETHANES ARE. LACQUERS ARE MORE WATER-RESISTANT THAN VARNISHES AND SHELLACS BUT ARE SUSCEPTIBLE TO CRACKING AND PEELING. ACID-CURING SWEDISH FINISHES ARE FAST-DRYING AND RESIST YELLOWING. PENETRATING FINISHES PRESERVE THE APPEARANCE OF THE GRAIN WHILE SOAKING INTO WOOD PORES. THEY ARE AN EFFECTIVE WAY TO COLOR A WOOD'S NATURAL GRAIN BUT, UNLIKE STAINS, THEY LEAVE A VERY THIN FILM AT THE SURFACE.

Top Left: Wide-plank softwood flooring in an elegant setting exudes warmth and timeless style. These floorboards are old-growth larch.

Top Right: Hardwood strips can be laid in a variety of directions and patterns for design interest.

Bottom Left: The iconic country kitchen has old, old pine flooring.

Bottom Right: The finish is an integral part of wood flooring's appearance. Here, softwood planks are protected with one of the new satin finishes now available in polyurethanes.

Hardwoods

Hardwood and Softwood

Softwoods

Above: from left to right, top to bottom: White Ash, American Birch, Chestnut, Elm, Gum, Hackberry, Pecan Hickory, Magnolia, Hard Maple, Black Walnut, and Yellow Poplar.

Right: from left to right, top to bottom: Baldcypress, Eastern White Pine, Southern Pin, and Heart Pine.

Parquet
and Inlay

The newest embellishments to wood floors aren't part of the wood itself but, rather, decorative images composed of aluminum oxide particles embedded into many layers of polyurethane. In other words, the embellishment is part of the finish. Patterns and colors usually only found in painted and stenciled floors come ready-made as tongue-and-groove planks in standard widths, ready to pop into an otherwise sober wood floor.

Parquet and inlay used to be the most deluxe of wood flooring. Now, laser technology is doing for inlay what designs embedded in the finish are doing to border stencils—providing more options at price points unheard of a short time ago.

The Latest Options

Many decorative wood inlays are still being made by highly skilled craftsmen, but the new laser-cutting techniques are reviving this classic design tradition. Individual components of the design can be constructed out of a variety of woods for three-dimensional effect. The parts are cut from 5/16-inch (.8 cm) hardwood and then joined with glue or urethane adhesive. When the inlay is dry, its edges are routed to match the tongue-and-groove joints of the rest of the floor, and the inlay is set in place. Additional drama can be created by dyeing components with aniline dyes; the color and contrast remains even after sanding.

Stock inlays are becoming plentiful, but laser-cutting technology also makes it easier to create custom designs. If you have a family crest, signature emblem, or classic favorite, it can be a rich part of the foyer floor. Some of the most popular stock designs available include center medallions and compass roses, southwestern patterns, floral and geometric borders, and a whole menagerie of animals. Any of them make fitting embellishments to the living or dining room floor, but consider how striking an oval decorative medallion might be on a stair landing. Or use a motif at the entrance to a room that signals its use.

Inlay can be used to guide the eye along a hallway or to create flow in an overall layout. Borders are popular ways of defining or stressing the definition of a room's footprint. When the border is inlaid in a different variety of wood, the effect tends to be richer and more architectural. Secondary wood varieties in the room can be beautifully echoed this way.

In both inlaid wood and finish-coat decorations, colorful designs featuring fruit and flowers are best suited to farmhouse and country interiors, while classic designs such as the Greek key can generally work in most decorative schemes. Be careful when using center medallions or other large designs. These work best in large rooms with more or less square outlines, but can easily overwhelm a small room or render an asymmetric one lopsided. Also be careful to avoid the room-shrinking effect of a border placed too far in from the walls. (Too close to the walls, on the other hand, makes it look stingy.) Before installing any kind of wood floor decoration, make a scale drawing with the decorative element also drawn to scale.

Left: Because technology has streamlined the manufacturing process, the designer-look of an imposing center medallion in the entry is now within the reach of most homeowners.

Right: Lavish border and center embellishments are now available as component parts that can be inserted into any floor.

Inlay Options

Ornate Medallion Inlay

Classic Medallion Inlay   Inlay Borders

Fruit, Diamond, and Grecian Key Inlays

Diamond-pattern Plank Inlay

Parquet Options

[PWF-P(2a – 2s)-FLO] this is all one file not individual images but they're labeled as requested

| Purple Heart | Santos Mahogany | Leopard Wood | Walnut | Red Oak | Maple | Bloodwood | Brazilian Cherry | American Cherry |

| Genuine Mahogany | Lace Wood | Ash | Bubinga | Wenge | Rosewood | Birds-eye Maple | White Oak | Padauk |

Paint
and Stencil

Lovers of wood flooring like to point out that there is no flooring type that is easier to transform completely, without the inconvenience of new construction and for minimal cost, than a wood floor. Paint can give new life to an old, worn floor or it can turn a raw new floor into a gently patinated one with the feel of an antique. You can apply an overall coat of literally any color paint for a quick fix for worn or discolored floors, and this is an economical way to finish new pine boards. Painting a floor provides an ideal opportunity to brighten or mute the room, bring a color scheme into focus, or to experiment with new color combinations.

With the right primer, old paint or finishes can usually be covered. However, flaking, chipping, or loose surface treatments should be sanded first. Many people like to use deck or boat paint on a floor, but you can use regular enamel or eggshell paints. Floors are best primed with acrylic paints that will flex with movement. After painting, the surface of the floor will be finished off with several coats of polyurethane, and you will probably want to refresh the polyurethane annually to protect the painted finish.

If you prefer a pattern to an overall coat, the tried-and-true geometric floor is an excellent design solution for a great variety of house styles, from Colonial antique to Country to Contemporary. It is achieved by careful measuring, taping, and then painting sections of the floor. The paint can be used to emulate stone, metal, leather, or any other material; a favored approach is to paint dramatically veined faux marble in contrasting light and dark colors. Or the floor can be a merry checkerboard of two favorite colors.

Another popular decorative approach to wood flooring is to stencil a pattern onto the overall floor or onto a specific area. Stenciled floors are most effective when designed to work with the room's architecture; you might want to echo or magnify a decorative element, to point out something about the style of the house, or to accentuate or minimize a floor plan. Many companies offer design, color, and technical advice, as well as ready-cut stencils. This is an indication of the fact that floor stenciling, when done with care, is a craft that even the inexperienced can carry out to great effect.

How to Stencil a Border on a Floor

Step 1: To square off a floor for stenciling, take the measurements of the floor and use them to draw a plan to scale on graph paper. Measure your stencil block and decide on an appropriate scale.

Step 2: Find and mark with chalk the centers of the walls and mark off the positions of the stencil pattern blocks, allowing for whatever space you choose between the wall and the stencil border.

Step 3: If one corner is cut off (with boxed-in pipes, for example), cut off the corner of the stenciled border and repeat this device for decorative consistency in each of the other three corners.

Step 4: If you want to add any stencils in the center of the floor, stretch a piece of heavily chalked string between the centers of both pairs of opposite walls. Where the two lines cross will be the center of the room. Working from the center, position any additional stencils at equal distances away from it.

Top Left: There is no more effective or economical way to completely change the look of a room than with a coat of paint. Here, the floor is wood, but other flooring can be painted as well.

Top Right: Even the simplest pattern stenciled onto a floor can become the basis for a decorative scheme for the entire room.

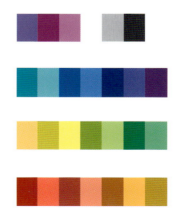

Mix and match colors to create stunning borders.

Floorcloths

Floorcloths are canvas "rugs" painted in imitation of fine flooring or carpeting as colorful and inexpensive alternatives. That is to say, they were. Today, floorcloths are highly desirable flooring in themselves, no longer considered second best. They are used like any area rug: in the hallway, in kitchens, in front of the fire. However, because floorcloths are painted canvas, they are not as durable as rugs or carpets, and they cannot be washed. Floorcloths aren't so fragile as to be impractical, however. You can walk on them, and usually a regular sweeping keeps them clean.

Floorcloths can look good in any décor, since there are no limits to their design inspiration. They are, however, a wonderfully authentic element in a country home, and many of the floorcloths offered for sale are decorated with country motifs.

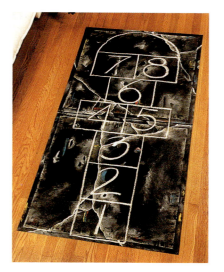

Top: There are no limits to design inspiration, including that of floorcloths. For starters, they don't have to be rectangular.

Left: There are no rules that say floorcloths have to be styled in country motifs.

Above: When making your own floorcloth, draw on your own life for ideas.

Mosaics

Mosaic is the name we give to the pictures or decorative designs that are made when small pieces of colored glass, stone, or tile are set into mortar. It's an ancient craft that's always being rediscovered. In its constant re-emergence as a decorative art, mosaic is like paint on a wall—familiar, even commonplace, until the materials enter the hands of a skilled artisan. Then, the artistic expression is as fresh and new as the imagination creating it.

The pieces of stone that make up mosaic flooring are quite small, so that mosaic really is a kind of painting with stone, and mosaic floors transcend the design limitations of the medium. Mosaics are essentially made the same way now as they were when they were the chic flooring material of choice in Pompeii. Small stone pieces are selected and set into mortar by hand. This surpassingly simple technique has design flexibility that constantly puts mosaic flooring at the cutting edge of interior fashion. It's no wonder that mosaics have always stood for status flooring—they can be created in any range of colors and patterns, and from ancient civilizations on, have been used to advertise the homeowner's power—or latest enthusiasm. It's no different today. Custom mosaic flooring is limitless in color and design; this is one way of getting exactly the floor you want.

Ready-Made Mosaics

Less costly is the option of inserting ready-made mosaics into floors to create borders or other decorative elements. A mesh background carries a design that can be laid into any type of flooring, though stone is most common. A classic Greek key, curling waves, vines, or autumn leaves might form the edge of a simple stone floor. With planning and preparation, you might also insert a mosaic decorative element into a ceramic tile or even wood floor, to become part of an overall material mix for the ultimate personal flooring statement.

You might use mosaics to create a colorful picture in the center of a kitchen floor, for example. A mosaic in the same color stone as an entry floor might scribe the initials of the homeowners for a subtle yet highly personal statement. Or consider the drama created when a glass mosaic element is introduced into honed marble; the reflective mosaic glitters like a jewel in the rich, matte surface. There really are no limitations; mosaics are as comfortable on a bathroom floor as they are in a formal living room.

Just as you can enrich an outfit with well-chosen accessories, so too can a floor be ornamented with mosaics. But stone pictures have more versatility than clothing accessories; they can take center stage to star in the dramatic composition. Few floors make as powerful a design statement as those whose entire surface is composed of colorful bits of stone. Consider mosaics as a flooring material if you want hardness and longevity combined with color and finely detailed pattern.

Above: Insert a mosaic border for a rich, luxurious statement. Such borders are now available as separate elements; they can be placed at the whim of the floor designer.

Left: Pretty pictures composed with small, colored stones—that's what mosaics are all about.

Mosaic Motifs

Mosaic Borders

Mosaic Florals and Foliage

Tile Style

For many rooms, tile is a beautiful and practical choice. When it comes to tile, ceramic is the classic. It cleans easily, is very durable, and is resistant to dampness. This makes it ideal for kitchens and baths, as well as vestibules and foyers—which may see a bit of water, snow, and mud during wet weather. But ceramic tile is only the beginning. What about vinyl, leather, cork, wood, concrete, plastic, and even glass? Following are some exciting ways to use tile in your home.

- Mix ceramic tiles with abandon. For a Mediterranean atmosphere, complement earthy terra-cotta tiles with a border of hand-painted or Mexican tiles for a unique blend of old-world flavor.

- Colored glass tiles give floors a subtle yet distinctive glow, and since they're made from bits of recycled glass, they will impress your environmentally conscious guests. You don't need to outfit a whole room in glass tile. Try them in a border treatment around a more traditional ceramic tile bathroom floor.

- Stone tiles—brick, slate, limestone, marble, and other natural materials—are perfect for low-maintenance, high-interest flooring in kitchens, baths, and even living rooms.

- Install colorful vinyl tiles in a checkerboard pattern to liven up a retro-styled kitchen. Vinyl tiles are an easy way for the do-it-yourselfer on a budget to give a room an entirely new look. Softer, less expensive, and easier to install than its ceramic, marble, and stone cousins, vinyl tile is manufactured in a wide variety of colors, patterns, and textures.

- Concrete tiles can be tinted to match countertops, cabinetry, even your favorite set of china, and they look great with today's restaurant-inspired kitchens. They're also durable and extremely low maintenance—an occasional damp-mopping will keep them looking stunning.

- Indulge in leather tiles to lend an air of sophistication to less traffic-heavy spaces. A rich leather floor can become the focal point of a living room, bedroom, or study.

Vinyl Composition Tile

Vinyl Composition Tile

Indian Ivory Limestone Tile

Vitreous Glass Mosaic Tile

Leather Floor and Wall Tile

Tile with the hand-thrown look of pottery works to create a dimensional field of color and soft pattern.

Linoleum Style

Linoleum, the first thoroughly modern flooring material, is the darling flooring of today's animal-rights activists and environmentalists. It is entirely made of natural, renewable materials: linseed oil, wood flour, ground cork, limestone, jute. It's handsome and comfortable. A bonus is the characteristic smell, which is the faint aroma of the flax seed or linseed oil—that's at the heart of this lovely product.

Linoleum was eclipsed by vinyl as a favorite flooring for much of the past fifty years, but it's making a strong comeback. Recent introductions of both jute and polyester-backed linoleum tile have brought about something new—do-it-yourself linoleum installation. It's tougher than vinyl; the curing process of linoleum continues long after installation, so that it gets harder and more durable with age.

Today's decorators favor linoleum in marbled and flecked solids, pieced to make graphic color and design statements. It's easy to cut, thus suiting it to smooth curves that aren't possible with most materials. Early color limitations have been largely eliminated, as have some of the more lurid florals of the past. Floor borders and corners are available as stock items in geometrics and classic motifs.

Linoleum is great in kitchens—comfortable for the cook, durable, and easy to clean. But don't think of it as merely utilitarian. Linoleum is good-looking, and can go wherever you want it to. ■ ■ ■

RECYCLE THE FLOOR

DUMPING AN OLD FLOOR? DO IT WITHOUT WORRY—IF IT'S LINOLEUM. ALL THE NATURAL INGREDIENTS IN LINOLEUM ARE BIODEGRADABLE, WHICH MEANS THEY WON'T CLOG UP THE LANDFILL FOREVER; THEY WILL SIMPLY DECAY AWAY. QUICKLY.

Left: Linoleum has astonishing longevity. Chic again, it has come full circle in our style sensibility. Along with that comes new appreciation for the old patterns.

Linoleum Options

Single-layer linoleum comes in a beautiful range of colors.

Marbled, flecked, and graphic patterns are newly popular.

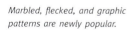  

Vinyl Style

With vinyl, floors entered the twentieth century. One hundred years later, it is solidly entrenched as a flooring favorite. Resilient, available at every price point in a vast array of colors and patterns, easy to install and care for—vinyl is truly for every home.

Because of its dominance in the flooring market, vinyl sheet or tile can be found to suit any style of interior. Contemporary manufacturing processes now use extreme heat and pressure to sculpt the surface of the material, producing texture for a particular design feature such as the grout of a tile or the pebbled surface of a stone design. Realistic visual appeal combined with vinyl's smooth resilience makes this the choice for homeowners who want the look for less combined with easy care. At the high end of the price spectrum, sheet vinyl floors are subtly colored and lavishly cushioned. And, keep in mind that vinyl tile flooring is easily installed by do-it-yourselfers.

A recent vinyl flooring introduction comes from Sweden, where it is used as the raw material for a woven wall-to-wall carpet. Vinyl fibers, which resemble the gimp you made lanyards from at summer camp, are machine-woven for a tough top layer, which is then bonded to a vinyl base. The result has greater texture and is softer than vinyl sheet or tile. It is extremely strong, water-resistant, and has the surface of woven fabric, but without the nap. It is available either in bold stripes of color, or in the tweeds created by two colors woven together.

At the high end, a vinyl floor costing as much as cork or wood can incorporate extra cushioning and sound-absorption features, along with designer patterns and colors. Most vinyl flooring is priced in the low and middle range. But designers newly enamored of vinyls and laminates (aka plastics) create across the board. There is very chic, very affordable vinyl flooring: Investigate 12-inch by 12-inch (30 cm by 30 cm) self-adhesive floor tiles in pale neutral shades, for instance.

The wildly popular wood laminate floor is, in fact, a close relative of vinyl flooring. The material has come a long way; vinyl flooring is a direct descendant of Bakelite, the first completely synthetic plastic, introduced in 1909. It was made and marketed during the early twentieth century as Vinylite.

Vinyl Options

Woven vinyl has a great texture and iron-clad durability.

Vinyl Composition Tile

Vinyl flooring can look like anything and go anywhere. At its best, it is so much a part of a room that nothing else could be imagined in its place.

Soft Flooring
Options

We have a craving for softness under our feet, especially in our homes. Soft flooring is easy on the back while we're standing, and it gives us visual cues that say "comfort." We can expect to keep seeing new developments until the possibilities of nearly every kind of material have been exhausted—and that won't happen as long as artists and designers keep having ideas.

Carpeting pile presents problems for allergy sufferers, but sometimes a vinyl floor just isn't natural enough. From Finland comes the Verso carpet. Linen fabric, which is extremely strong, is woven through birch slats, with the two materials forming the warp and the woof of the carpet. The results look like a hand-woven cotton or wool rug, with the protruding ends of the birch slats forming the fringe. Since the birch elements are extremely thin, the carpeting has much more flexibility than you'd expect. Patterns have a bold Scandinavian look that's perfect for modern interiors or for folkloric design schemes.

Leather tiles make a floor that's comfortable, atmospheric, and surprisingly long wearing. Now, a new line of leather flooring tile has brought color. Aniline dyes, far-removed from the shoe-polish-like leather stains of the past, produce saturated colors like terra-cotta reds, forest greens, ochre yellows, as well as more traditional oxblood and saddle colors. A great choice for libraries or dens, leather flooring is moving into bedrooms, where its sound-absorption is especially appreciated.

Left: Cork is perennially among our favorites for soft flooring; painting or stenciling it adds whole new design possibilities.

Right: Carpets are always in vogue but can always look new.

Beautiful Bamboo

Think of the design potential of a bamboo floor. The perennial grass favored by pandas, bamboo encompasses a huge family of plants, some of which are ideal for flooring. While strong (it looks like hardwood), bamboo flooring has the pale coloration we associate with this plant, as well as the characteristic protruded ringed joints, known as knuckles. The effect is perfectly suited to an Asian-inspired interior, or to a design scheme that seeks to emphasize natural materials. Environmentalists are especially fond of bamboo for flooring because it is a renewable resource.

The latest evolution in bamboo flooring is an engineered product called plyboo, in which wood laminates are faced with a top wear layer of bamboo. It is not inexpensive and makes a versatile product.

Left: Leather flooring, beautiful and fragrant, is surprisingly tough.

Right: The sound-deadening characteristics of leather floor tiles make them especially popular in bedrooms, living rooms, or anywhere else where quiet, luxury, and softness are appreciated.

A Range in Leather

Defining Space
with Flooring

Floors are unique. They do double duty as structural and as decorative parts of a home. As such, they must be designed around your needs and wishes. Floor designers will often focus on the floor's structural strength to the exclusion of other important considerations. Once you know what your many design options are, you can work with your designer to get a floor that is structurally sound and aesthetically pleasing.

Use your floors to define space. Once you start to think outside the limits of floors as background, you open up design possibilities that can improve the function of the rooms in your house. People automatically set their feet on the flooring that appears to be most comfortable and stable; use this knowledge consciously, and your home's traffic patterns will make sense, regardless of the size of the living area.

An often-mentioned problem for modern homeowners is a cramped entrance to their homes. If your floor leads the eye into an adjoining room, perhaps flowing in and becoming a part of it, a small entryway will seem larger.

Sometimes the opposite creates a problem—an open expanse of floor leaves visitors without directional signals; they literally don't know which way to turn. Think of this as an opportunity to use pattern. By creating visual pathways, you'll lead guests in the direction you'd like them to go.

Of course, structural strength is important; combined with beauty, it makes the best floor.

Top Left: Once you think outside of predictable parameters, you can use floors to define space in exciting ways.

Top Right: A small entry can be visually enlarged through the use of the right flooring.

Bottom Left: Give visual and tactile clues to those entering your home.

Bottom Right: How a floor feels and sounds are part of what helps determine traffic patterns.

Tactile sensations send equally important signals. A smooth, resilient floor that changes to a softer carpet underfoot shows us the boundaries between the kitchen's areas of use; the cook stands on the smooth floor while guests congregate in the cozy corner. Similarly, a carpet defines the conversation area in a living room with polished marble floors. In these cases, form follows function—the carpet protects the mirrorlike surface of the stone and the business end of the kitchen is easy to clean.

Two types of flooring material signal change in use as well as visually separating space.

Choose your materials with thought. The simplest element can make a strong statement on the floor; you need not spend a large amount of money to produce an interesting and imaginative effect. When nailing down soft pine boards, for instance, you might space the nails in a pattern, or you might precolor the wood plugs that are commonly used to cover them. The result can be compelling: Imagine a wide-board softwood floor, with its characteristic knots and color variations, marked with a grid of blue dots. Needless to say, the plugs (boatbuilders call them bungs) will be most effective if they echo the room's architecture, play up a color scheme, or lead the eye toward a focal point or into the next room.

Does your new house look a little too new? The single best way to give it that lived-in atmosphere is with flooring. Explore the varieties of recycled old floorboards now on the market. Older flooring often comes in wide widths, a feature appreciated by many homeowners. A number of companies offer the floors that were once in industrial buildings, but some of this type of flooring comes from more exotic places. Pine logs that have spent 150 years submerged in riverbeds, for instance, are the source for a particularly lovely patinated wood floorboard.

A modern kitchen is up a set of marble steps; in the kitchen, the floor changes to wood.

Top: The dining room of a brand new house achieves the gentle patina of age through the use of old, recycled floorboards.

Left: Material creates atmosphere. Here, metal stairs make a space that is streamlined, spare, open, and modern.

Top: Classic does not mean dull. Imaginative flooring will look good in the long term while remaining stylish.

Left: Think it through; your favorite, most personal way of creating an interior includes the floor.

Floors Last a Lifetime

Keep one thing in mind: Your floors should last for the life of the house, and you may tire of any overtly trendy flooring statement long before its natural life is over. You will also want to give some consideration to possible future changes in décor. This is not to say that your floors should be neutral, dull 'go with everything' compromises. Some of the most beautiful, classic flooring options are also the most versatile. But, if you install a floor composed of large limestone slabs, for example, it is unlikely that you'll want to replace it. If you get tired of it, which is also unlikely, the best you'll be able to do is to cover it with something.

A carefully considered floor isn't one you'll want or need to re-do periodically. Design your floor for the long term, and it will give you renewed pleasure every day.

No matter how small, a carpet can create an area entirely separate from the rest of the room. Here is a small oasis for rest and reflection.

Sophisticated Surfaces

Sin ser faro ni roca
I AM NOT A LIGHTHOUSE OR A ROCK,
En medio del mar estoy,
BUT LIVE AT THE END OF THE SEA,
Tambien estoy en la playa:
YOU'LL ALSO FIND ME IN THE SAND
¡Adivinen, pues, quien soy!
NOW—GUESS WHO I MIGHT BE.

Un Caracol – a Seashell

Faux and Fantasy Finishes

Painting surfaces is not a new idea—even prehistoric people painted images on cave walls. Modern techniques, however, are rooted in traditions shaped during the Italian Renaissance in fifteenth-century Europe, painted traditions emulated and expanded upon to this day.

Contemporary American decorative artists use modern tools and materials to interpret age-old techniques—marbleizing, graining, glazing, and the like. Today's artists, however, move beyond traditional methods to create fantasy finishes and textures—cracked linens and textured wall surfaces among them. At times, the end result references natural materials; at times the finished surface captures pure fantasy.

In the following section, you'll find an example of very traditional faux bois rosewood, meticulously painted by the artists to imitate the richness of natural rosewood. By contrast, you'll also appreciate surface treatments inspired by color and texture, conceptual ideas rendered by the artist with honesty and integrity.

Photos: (background) courtesy of Ellen Lemer Korney;
(clockwise from top) Daniel McManus Photography; Chris
Covey; Peter Simon Photography; Isaac Bailey
Photography; Randy McCaffery Photography

Bopas

Tradition and craftsmanship characterize sophisticated painted finishes by Gedes Paskauskas and Robert Grady, partners in Bopas Studio in Boston, Massachusetts. Graduates of the School of the Worcester Art Museum, the partners apply their in-depth knowledge of color theory and application of pigment to their trade as decorative artists. Exquisite finishes unique to Bopas result. There is a natural translucence to their work, a richness that reveals itself through layers of skillfully applied paints and varnishes. This is especially apparent in their innovative rendering of standard wall and wood finishes. "Our inspiration comes from the beauty of the wood or material we're trying to recreate," says Grady, who understands that the most successful techniques are understated. The objective is to harmonize, not compete, with other elements in the room. Bopas employs six full-time artists, each trained in the fine arts. Paskauskas and Grady believe this distinction accounts for the inspired application of painted finishes for which Bopas is known.

Facing page:

Detail, Faux Bois Library

A soft sheen reminiscent of polished natural rosewood harmonizes with hand-painted Chinese wall murals and helps to create a mood of elegance.

Photos by Bruce T. Martin

Several layers of paint and varnish were applied to achieve graining characteristics of natural rosewood. In the darkest sections, intense markings flow back and forth; light and dark areas line up in a staccato fashion with areas of deep amber glowing through to the surface.

PASKAUSKAS AND GRADY PREPARE THE EXISTING MAHOGANY AND poplar surfaces by applying a base coat of an intense amber color. The amber glows through each succeeding layer of varnish and replicates the natural glow of exotic, high-quality rosewood. With their training as fine artists, the partners understand how to manipulate color, value, and line to reproduce a natural grained effect with oil paints, artist colors, and varnishes.

The partners were responsible for all the finishes here, from graining bookshelves, crown molding, chair rail, wainscoting, audiovisual built-in unit, and mantle, to glazing the ceiling and gilding details. They chose a ragging treatment for the ceiling, glazing the entire surface in a celadon green. The subtle yellowish-green tones of the celadon complement the soft amber glow of the rosewood, polished to a satiny sheen with a mixture of rotten stone and oil. To create this harmonious whole, the artists were inspired by the natural qualities of exotic rosewood and by fabrics and hand-painted Chinese wall murals chosen by the designer.

Maintaining the tonal consistency of faux bois is a challenge when applying the painted finish to several surfaces in one room. This audio-visual unit plus bookshelves, moldings, chair rail, wainscoting, and mantle are rendered in faux bois rosewood.

1

Faux Bois Rosewood
Paskauskas and Grady achieve the warm glow and distinctive markings of rosewood through skillful manipulation of glazes and painstaking attention to detail.

2
Deep amber is the base color of faux bois rosewood by Bopas.

3
The artists apply custom-mixed glazes—a combination of Vandyke brown and black artist colors—to lay in the overall patterning of the grain.

4
Using a small sable brush, the artists articulate the characteristics of rosewood's distinctive graining.

A Gallery of Surfaces by Bopas

As artists, we enjoy the challenge of developing a wall finish that first uses color to set off the objects in the room, and then uses a textural motif to animate the surface.

**Gedes Paskauskas and
Robert Grady**

"Tuscany" Wall Mural

Inspired by Tuscan gardens, Paskauskas and Grady use acrylic wall paints and artist colors to render this mural, measuring 11.5 feet by 14 feet (3.5 meters by 4.3 meters). Blue sky completes the illusion of indoor/outdoor, activating a plain windowless wall.

***Detail*, "Tuscany" Wall Mural**

A tiny painted butterfly flits on the painted surface, lending reality to illusion.

***Detail*, "Tuscany" Wall Mural**

A plaster cast replica of a Michelangelo sculpture is inspiration for the artists' realistic detailing. With the exception of the chair rail 30 inches (76 centimeters) from the floor, the entire wall surface is painted by Bopas.

Photos, this page by Daniel McManus Photography

Striped Walls

Using a base coat of creamy off-white, Paskauskas and Grady stripe the walls using a vibrant yellow glaze, transforming a dark narrow hallway into a bright sunny area.

Photos, this page by Daniel McManus Photography

Detail, Striped Walls

To stripe the walls, the artists first apply the background color of creamy off-white, then tape the walls, and finally use a brush to glaze the now-isolated stripes.

Sitting Room

Reminiscent of Chinese Tea Paper, this beautifully subtle wall treatment is rendered by a "resist" method unique to Bopas. Glazing a pale yellow/ocher over a pale yellow base, Paskauskas presses lace saturated with solvent into semi-dry glaze. After manipulating the surface, he pulls the fabric away to reveal a series of distinctive impressions.

Photo by Sam Gray Photography
Design by Susan Neddich

Detail, Sitting Room

The "resist" method developed by Paskauskas and Grady effectively mimics the look of Chinese Tea Paper and introduces a softness to their painted surfaces.

Photo courtesy of Bopas

Facing page:

Garden Room

Drawing inspiration from early nineteenth-century
itinerant painters, the artists apply their palette
of "dirty" colors—yellow ochers, gray greens,
burnt oranges—to render this garden room with
faded florals and stucco-like wall surface darkened
with age.

Photo by Bruce T. Martin

High Victorian Wall Treatment

Paskauskas and Grady painstakingly apply hunter
green and ocher glazes to the detailing on the existing
plaster relief walls, replicating the original Victorian
era wall covering.

Photos, this page by Daniel McManus Photography

Detail, **High Victorian Wall Treatment**

Pomegranate detailing is evident on this relief
plaster wall surface recreated in original colors
by the artists.

Joe Fenzl

Twenty years of experience in Santa Monica, California place Joe Fenzl in the forefront of a field that he describes as "a combination of art and craft." Fenzl accurately describes his own exquisitely crafted, painterly decorative techniques. Much of his success is rooted in his knowledge of materials. "If you're not using the correct materials," he says, "you might get a particular finish, but it might not hold up."

Fenzl's color choice and the way in which he approaches his textural finishes reveal his classic sensibilities. He wants his work to fit into the contemporary world yet "remain in style," he says.

Fenzl demonstrates his expertise by using a wide variety of surface materials in creative ways. Always adding to his repertoire, he continually tries new techniques. His series of textural papers for walls is one of Fenzl's innovative contributions to the field of contemporary decorative arts.

Detail, Column, Kitchen Breakfast Bar
Using the same process as with the breakfast bar wall, Fenzl glazes and seals the cement column, transforming an otherwise unattractive detail into a stunningly simple architectural element.

MY CHALLENGE WAS TO CREATE HARMONY IN THIS CALIFORNIA beach condo. Its small size—only 1,200 square feet (108 square meters)—added to the challenge, as did the way in which wall surfaces visually interconnected. The client wanted a contemporary look. To comply, I rendered existing concrete and wood surfaces in soft, textural finishes. I borrowed my palette from nature—muted earth tones, taupe, caramel colors and wood tones—and, playing off the views of sky and sea, I chose muted aqua as an accent color.

Moving from the central kitchen through to the living room, which is separated only by a breakfast bar, and down a short hallway to the master bath, I rendered several complementary surface finishes. In effect, the walls became an unobtrusive backdrop for a condo with spectacular views of the Pacific Ocean—I saw no need to compete with Mother Nature.

Facing page:

Kitchen Breakfast Bar
The concrete wall forming the base of the breakfast bar, and separating kitchen from living room, provides Fenzl with a challenge, which he meets with characteristic aplomb. The artist applies a very, very light aqua glaze to a smooth top layer of cement to achieve an unobtrusive mottled effect..

Photos by Dan Fenzl

Living Room Wall: Distressed Textural Stria

The artist drags a dry brush through a wet acrylic textural paste, which he applies to the wall surface in four-foot wide sections. An application of deerskin taupe glaze followed by a glaze of golden rust accents the stria effect of the brushstrokes.

Photos by Dan Fenzl

Door: Faux Bois, Teak

To contrast with a baseboard of light natural teak wood, Fenzl renders all condo doors in a dark teak faux bois by combing glazes over a medium tan painted ground. A clear glaze tinted with a brown aniline dye simulates the depth of actual teakwood.

Master Bath: Polished Plaster Marble Lustro finish

Tinting Marble Lustro with an earthy taupe, Fenzl trowels his textural wall formula on the walls. After smooth troweling a second layer tinted linen-white, he uses fine steel wool to apply a mixture of beeswax and carnuba wax, which he buffs to a satin sheen. The double layer of Marble Lustro, in complementary pigments, gives the depth of coloration.

A Gallery of Surfaces by Joe Fenzl

Many things influence me. . . .

Nature inspires many of my

textures and surfaces—stones,

the barks of trees. And European

antiquity—old worn plasters

patinaed with age. . . .

Joe Fenzl

Kitchen Cupboard
The artist interprets a look of Italian Tuscany by painting several layers of bone white over a dark stain, sanding back through the layers, and applying an umber finish glaze. Random water marking, a technique whereby fast-drying solvent is spattered sparingly onto the finished piece, adds subtle nuances. Highlighting edges with an oil colorant tinted with raw umber, he clear coats to finish.

Textural Papers for Wall Surfaces

In creating his series of textural papers for wall surfaces, Fenzl uses processes similar to decorative techniques he developed for direct application of materials onto walls. For ease of rolling and subsequent application of his exquisitely rendered, custom-designed, handmade wallpapers to a wall, he builds his textural surfaces using only flexible materials.

"Stone"

Onto kraft paper, the artist trowels two layers of a textural acrylic—the first tinted gray, the second tinted cream. A final glazing with umber gives the textured paper its canyon color.

Photos by Dan Fenzl

"Frottage"

After applying white paint to butcher paper, Fenzl brushes the surface with glue. When dry, he applies mossy green water-base paint, which reacts with the water soluble glue to create a crackle finish. He then manipulates the wet paint, exposing the background randomly. A raw umber finish glaze creates the patina.

Bottom this page and facing page top:

"Ceramic"

Onto white butcher paper, the artist applies a thin layer of acrylic textural material tinted caramel. He then applies a crackle medium to create the eggshell texture. Next, a caramel glaze establishes a soft alabaster color which is finished with a clear coat.

"Porcelain"

With a base of butcher paper, Fenzl randomly trowels on a layer of Marble Lustro, a semi-translucent textural material developed by the artist. A charcoal-colored glaze applied after the crackle medium creates the Raku color of the final paper.

"Leather"

By gluing tissue paper onto kraft paper, the artist creates a wrinkled-up surface similar in appearance to coarse leathers. He paints the textural surface cream, glazes in tan, and establishes an overall tonal quality called "Bombay" by applying a clear finish coat tinted slightly with brown aniline dye.

"Strata"

The artist trowels two layers of acrylic textural material onto kraft paper, the first tinted light charcoal, and the second tinted antique white. Two layers of glazes follow, one peach and the other a charcoal gray. Vertical application of materials contributes to the stone-like effect of the bison-colored surface.

"Antique Gold"

Fenzl applies a thick layer of acrylic textural material to wrinkle the kraft paper base. After applying gold leaf, he partially paints the surface with a thin layer of taupe acrylic. When dry, he glazes the surface and finishes it with a clear coat, water-based acrylic tinted with an earthy brown aniline dye, which gives it its antique gold finish.

"Block" Wall

Fenzl stiples his brush across wet plaster to achieve pitted areas similar to the textures of natural travertine. Simultaneously, the entire surface is scored into blocks. To achieve his desired palette, he glazes a background of light cream in sand tones.

Photo by Chris Covey

Interior design, this page and facing by Ellen Lemer Korney

Facing page:

Pool House

Recreating a Pompeii distressed plaster, the artist applies a coat of drywall compound to the walls. He then rubs pigment into the compound, sanding back randomly and sealing with shellac. His palette is Italian-ocher, chrome green, and Pompeii red with a black band to accent.

Photo courtesy of Ellen Lemer Korney

Painted Surfaces

The history of modern painted furniture parallels the history of faux finishes, periods of artistic experimentation focusing on interior decor. The aesthetic sensibility that appreciated the fine art of painted furniture continues to evolve as artists boldly encourage clients to experiment with their environments.

In Europe, elaborately painted furniture in the courts and palaces of the nobility made its appearance three centuries ago. Initially the artist's intent was to imitate natural materials, an extension of the faux finishes applied to wall surfaces and architectural detailing. Later, the furniture became something of a three-dimensional canvas onto which artists painted scenes and decorations. Oriental lacquered furniture first made its appearance when Europe and America began trade with the Far East. These elaborately and exquisitely painted and gilded pieces of furniture had an enormous influence on generations of artists and crafts-people in the West.

Today, anything goes. In this section, you will find artists engaged in executing a variety of methods and approaches from painting furniture to complement fabric, to simulating marble on a fireplace hearth.

Photos: (background) James M. Goodnough Photography;
(clockwise from top) Jim Stob Photographer; Jim Stob
Photographer; Vince Valdez; James M. Goodnough
Photography; Kelli Ruggere Photography; James M.
Goodnough Photography

Dining Room Table

Adding a wide whitewashed stripe and hand-painted woodbine leaves and currant-colored berries to a simple pine table, the artists borrow their palette from the chair coverings. For consistency, the artists carry the design onto the dining chairs.

Photo by James M. Goodnough Photography

Dale Wade and Helen Doane

Cape Cod, Massachusetts artists Dale Wade and Helen Doane combine their talents, sometimes working together, sometimes individually. It all depends on individual client needs and the complexity and size of a commission. The two women credit a trompe l'oeil class taught by the late Heather Braginton-Smith, a talented artist and gifted teacher, as the defining moment in the development of their decorative arts career.

Wade and Doane share many skills, an ability to simplify being one. This is most apparent when the artists coordinate painted finishes with existing design elements, fabrics in particular. Rather than reproducing draperies, upholstery, or bed linen designs in what can be distracting detail, Wade's and Doane's painted surfaces complement existing fabrics. Additionally, the artists share a sophisticated sense of color, critical to matching paints to dyes. After almost a decade in business, Wade and Doane render faux finishes and trompe l'oeil techniques in addition to decorative painting.

Dining Room Chair
In a simple yet effective gesture, the artists add decorative designs to the back of production-line dining chairs, pulling their palette from the seat coverings.

Photo by Dale Michaels Wade

WE'VE FOUND SUCCESSFUL DECORATIVE PAINTING DOESN'T mean covering an entire surface with paint. This pine dining table, with its wide whitewashed striped and hand-painted woodbine leaves and currant-colored berries, illustrates the elegance of simplicity.

Our greatest challenge with this project was to find an innovative way to expand the seating capacity of this dining table from six to ten. Our solution was to build a "topper," or "tabletop mural" that would hang on the dining room wall until needed. We decided to paint a local scene, working from our original photograph. Then we painted trompe l'oeil window mullions and draperies to complete the illusion. Until pressed into action, the topper hangs behind the dining table and provides a "view" to the outside world.

Dining Room Table "Topper"

Painting from an original photograph of a local scene, the artists view the "topper" as a huge "canvas." Trompe l'oeil window mullions and draperies complete the illusion. Until pressed into action, the topper hangs behind the dining table and provides a "view" to the outside world.

Photo by Dale Michaels Wade

A Gallery of Surfaces by Dale Wade and Helen Doane

Each project presents unique challenges. We're inspired by several things—our customers' objectives, the final function of the piece or space in which we're working, tangible influences such as fabric and architecture, together with our two separate artistic sensibilities working together.

Dale Wade and Helen Doane

Detail, Room Screen

Wade paints a bronze-colored fence to create dimension on the three-paneled room divider. She adds vines using a combination of hand painting and stenciling.

Game Table, Fishing Theme

Doane confines herself to single themes when painting decorative game tables. Here, a fishing theme features "sand," fishing nets, bits of seaweed, a broken crab claw, mussel and scallop shells, and a fish hook "caught" in the net.

Photos, right and below left by James M. Goodnough Photography

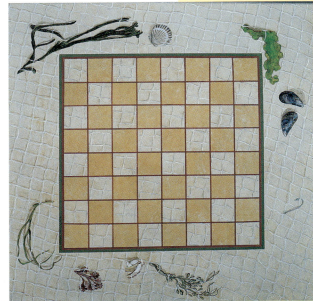

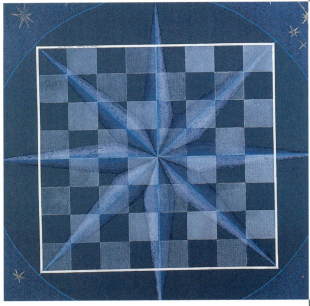

Game Table, Nautical Theme

A compass rose, painted in shades of cerulean and indigo, adds sparks of deep color. In keeping with a celestial motif and complementing the room's nautical theme, Doane paints gold stars around the edge of the game table.

Game Table, Hunting Theme

Wade paints a faux leather border in a rich burgundy color. Corner detailings accentuate the hunting theme.

Photo by Dale Michaels Wade

Detail, Pedestal Table

Doane borrows her palette, styling, and use of gold leaf from motifs popularized during the China Trade of the ninteenth century.

Bedroom Furniture

Wade accomplishes her cross-combing technique by brushing a bright sunny yellow glaze in one direction, and a soft buttery yellow in another. The overall effect is textural, yet doesn't compete with designs that Wade adds to her surface finishes—blue ribbon entwined with seaform green leaves on the game table, lattice panels on the armoire.

Pedestal Table

Doane renders Oriental designs and 23-carat gold leafing in a manner reminiscent of decorative styles prevalent during the China Trade in the early to mid 1800s.

Detail, Bedroom Furniture

When designing the headboard, Wade pulls decorative elements from the other pieces in the room, although she opts to paint them in what she calls a "small print" motif.

Photos, this page by James M. Goodnough Photography

Coffee Table and Tinware

Helen Doane transforms a simple wooden chest into a conversation piece by painting faux brick sides and adding ivy and an exquisite blue butterfly. Doane's hand-painted tin boxes and trays add decorative interest to a cozy corner and provide her client with an instant "collection."

Photos, right and below left by James M. Goodnough Photography

Tray: Nineteenth-century American Toleware design

Doane frames this authentic nineteenth-century American floral design with a 23-carat gold leaf border. The rose, morning glory, and other flowers are common features on Victorian era Toleware, from which Doane borrows her palette and technique.

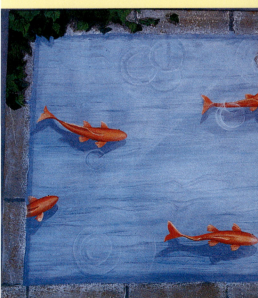

Floorcloth

Wade transforms a simple cotton canvas into a "goldfish pond" floorcloth.

Photo by Dale Michaels Wade

Detail, Trompe l'oeil Panel

Trompe l'oeil Cabinet

Wade adds a bit of whimsy to a trompe l'oeil panel, rendering a faux bois cabinet featuring fishing lures, books, and paraphernalia, and a very believable photo "taped" to the door.

Photos by James M. Goodnough Photography

Kitchen Bureau

Juxtaposing an imaginative color palette, the artist transforms a large awkward piece bureau into fine art furniture.

Kathy McDonald

Kathy McDonald thinks back to childhood when she thinks of her first dabblings into painting and decorating. Painting is now woven into the very fabric of her life: today more than ever, considering that McDonald's current challenge is to paint surfaces to match or complement fabrics in a client's home.

A certified decorative artist through the National Society of Toll and Decorative Painters, McDonald's style is joyful and refreshingly simple. She conceals any complexities from her viewers. Delightful decorative finishes and designs result as she juxtaposes her imaginative palette with a playfulness that engages the eye.

The artist's decade-plus-old Chicago business is very much word of mouth. McDonald works for individual clients and through interior designers—which, in fact, she herself is. The dual designation—interior designer/decorative artist—serves her well as she collaborates with clients, helping them to create their own unique environments.

Detail, Kitchen Bureau
The artist paints every square inch of this large kitchen bureau, adding color accents and detailing according to her detailed design sketch.

IN ITS RAW STATE, THIS KITCHEN BUREAU WAS TOO BIG AND TOO unattractive. But I saw it and knew immediately—here was a chance to make a statement.

I clipped pictures from magazines and asked my clients to show me ones that attracted their attention. A "blueprint" of their stylistic preferences and palette developed as they responded to geometries, bright colors, and metallics. With this valuable information in hand, I made a sketch and color board for their approval.

I used creative color combinations—purples, periwinkle, turquoise blues, golds, teals, coppers, and pearlized paints and metallics—to make our design statement. In executing, I penciled or taped individual sections. The inevitable irregularities where I followed pencil lines and painted freehand added to the charm of this piece, which I call "contemporary funk."

Believing details make a difference, I sculpted knobs from clay, pushing little metallic stones into the material when it was still soft. Later I painted them to accent the existing color story. And to add to the illusion of my painted "tiles," I masked off grout lines before I applied the high-gloss polyurethane to the entire piece.

***Detail,* Kitchen Bureau**

To lend an air of authenticity to her painted tiles, the artist tapes grout lines before applying a coat of high-gloss polyurethane to finish.

***Detail,* Kitchen Bureau**

Using pencil lines as guides, the artist paints various sections freehand, a technique that adds to the primitive charm of the piece.

A Gallery of Surfaces by Kathy McDonald

My clients inspire me. I look around and build on what I see in their homes, the styles they prefer. . . . I try to complement and coordinate my style with theirs. A decorative artist is a different kind of artist, and it's a different kind of process.

Kathy McDonald

Detail, Kitchen Hutch, knobs
Using a clay-like craft material, the artist sculpts and paints drawer knobs in keeping with the playful and casual ambiance of the piece.

Kitchen Hutch
Painting subtle checks and stripes in butter yellows and apple greens, the artist transforms an old secondhand kitchen hutch into a work of art. In keeping with the casual aspects of the piece, McDonald works freehand from penciled lines.

Detail, Kitchen Border, bird

The artist's interest in detailing is evident with her addition of this exquisitely painted bird, which has ostensibly "escaped" from the open door of the painted bird cage.

Kitchen Border, bird cage

Pulling navy blue and burgundies from fabrics in an adjoining room, the artist renders her freehand painted border design.

Detail, Laundry Room

Concerned about the inevitable moisture in the laundry room, the artist, who works in acrylics, seals her walls and decorative elements with a low-gloss polyurethane.

Laundry Room

Challenged to expand a cramped laundry room space, McDonald invites the outdoors in. There is a certain neoclassic look to the wall treatment with its potted plants and views of English gardens.

Wallcovering Resources

This alphabetical list of wallcovering manufacturers is furnished for your convenience. The addresses give the headquarters where you can obtain additional information about their products. Every attempt has been made to provide correct and up-to-date information. However, since addresses, telephone area codes, and Web sites are added or changed, there can be no guarantee the information remains accurate.

Keep in mind that new wallcovering patterns are constantly being introduced to replace others being retired. Should a particular pattern in this book inspire you, make sure that the wallcovering manufacturers have it in stock and available.

Agnes Bourne Studios
2 Henry Street
San Francisco, CA 94103
Phone: 415-626-6883
Fax: 415-626-2489
Web site: www.agnesbourne.com
E-mail: agnesbourne@sirius.com

Agnes Bourne Studios represents manufacturers of classic modern design to the trade only. Anya Larkin is represented in their showroom. Complete interior design services are available.

Barnaby Prints, Inc.
673 Jersey Avenue, P.O. Box 98
Greenwood Lake, NY 10925
Telephone: 914-477-2501
Fax: 914-477-2739
E-mail: 102775.564@
compuserve.com

Barnaby Prints produces custom wallpapers and borders hand printed exclusively for design firms.

Brunschwig & Fils
979 Third Avenue
New York, NY 10022-1234
Telephone: 212-838-7878
Fax: 212-371-3026
Web site: www.brunschwig.com
E-mail: hqr@brunschwig.com

Brunschwig & Fils is an international design studio recognized for their high-end custom-printed wallcoverings, in addition to their interior design services. Their contemporary and historically inspired wallcoverings can be seen at any of their nineteen showrooms located in the U.S., Canada, and the U.K. A recently published book, Brunschwig & Fils Style, *by Murray Douglas, presents a rich portfolio of their design projects.*

Chesapeake Wallcoverings
Corporation
401-H Prince George's Boulevard
Upper Marlboro, MD 20774
Telephone: 800-275-2037
Fax: 800-929-1169
Web site: www.cheswall.com
E-mail: info@cheswall.com

Chesapeake Wallcoverings offers a large selection of popular patterns, many ideal for a country decor. Their Web site functions as a frequently changed showroom.

Cole & Son—Distributed
by Whittaker & Woods
501 Highland Parkway
Smyrna, GA 30082
Telephone: 800-395-8760
Fax: 770-432-6215

Cole & Son's wood block printed wallpapers and hand-prints are sold internationally. Their line includes some of the finest archive wallpapers available.

Cowtan & Tout
Design Studio
979 Third Avenue
New York, NY 10022
Telephone: 212-753-4488
Fax: 212-593-1839

Cowtan & Tout is an international design firm, headquartered in London. Wallcoverings are high-end custom prints, many with matching fabrics. Their design studio in New York is open to the trade.

Decorating Den Interiors
Deborah Broughton
19100 Montgomery Village Avenue
Suite 200
Montgomery Village, MD 20886
Telephone: 800-332-3367
Fax: 301-272-1520
Web site: www.decoratingden.com

Decorating Den offers franchises to decorators, each independently owned and operated. Although not a manufacturer, Decorating Den has established accounts with all the major wallcovering companies, which makes them, in effect, a distributor of a wide range of brands. Wallcoverings, fabrics, furnishings, and decorating services are available throughout the U.S., Canada, and the U.K.

Photos for Decorating Den Interiors credited as follows: p. 26, Terri Ervin and Judith Slaughter, Allied ASID, DDCD; p. 38, top left, photo by D. Randolph Foulds, design by Laura Bowman-Messick and Lisa Tripp Hall; p. 45, top left, photo by Richard W. Green, design by Monique Barnum; p. 46, top left, photo by Bradley Olman, design by Judith Slaughter; p. 49, top, photo by Carolyn Abacheli, design by Tonie Vander Hulst, Allied ASID; p. 52, photo by Jackie Noble Azan, design by Carole Andrews, Anita Wiklem, and Nicolette Zaslow; p. 73, photo by Bradley Olman, design by Judith Slaughter.

Eisenhart Wallcoverings Co.
400 Pine Street P.O. Box 464
Hanover, PA 17331
Telephone: 800-931-WALL
Fax: 717-632-0288

Eisenhart Wallcoverings provides handsome, classically styled wallcoverings, borders, and fabrics available internationally.

Eisenhart's design center calls on a wealth of historic documents that also licenses designs to museums such as the Victoria and Albert Museum in London and the Smithsonian Institution in Washington, D.C.

FSC Wallcoverings
Includes FSC Contract, Gramercy, Greff, Schumacher, Village, Waverly, and Williamsburg.

See Schumacher & Company

Gramercy
79 Madison Avenue
New York, NY 10016
Telephone: 212-213-7795
Fax: 212-213-7640

Gramercy offers affordable, distinctive, transitional, and contemporary wallcoverings and fabrics. The focus is on high style with colors that are intriguing but safe. Designs are rendered with extraordinary beauty and care. Available through most paint and paper stores and home decorating retailers. Licensed collections include Christian Dior.

Greff
79 Madison Avenue
New York, NY 10016
Telephone: 800-988-7775
Web site: www.fsco.com

Self-described as an uptown designer brand, Greff is targeted at the designer trade through Schumacher showrooms. Eighteenth- and nineteenth-century American designs are predominantly featured.

Harlequin—Distributed
by Whittaker & Woods
5100 Highlands Parkway
Smyrna, GA 30082
Telephone: 800-395-8760
Fax: 770-432-6215

Harlequin's contemporary and transitional wallpaper and vinyl wallcovering prints and patterns are sold internationally. Some patterns have matching fabrics available.

Imperial Wallcoverings
23645 Mercantile Road
Beechwood, OH 44122
Telephone: 800-222-5044
Fax: 216-292-3206
Web site: www.imp-wall.com

Imperial wallcoverings are widely distributed and popular with the do-it-yourself market. Patterns are fashionable, with many geared toward the bedroom, bath, and kitchen, and are available through most paint and paper stores, home centers, and retail outlets catering to home furnishings.

Jolie Papier
8000 Cooper Avenue, Building #1
Glendale, NY 11385
Telephone: 718-894-8810
Fax: 718-894-9725

Jolie Papier, Ltd., markets their wallcovering and borders to both the residential and commercial marketplaces. Product classifications include 27" (69 cm) and 54" (137 cm) Type I and II fabric-backed wallcovering. Jolie Papier also produces an upper-end residential hand printed collection. Their brands are sold throughout the U.S., Canada, and the Pacific Rim. Patterns are generally available for four years.

Sanderson
285 Grand Avenue
3 Patriot Center
Englewood, NJ 07631
Telephone: 201-894-8400
Fax: 201-894-8871

Sanderson patterns are stylish, many with coordinating fabrics. Their offices are located in New York, Paris, and London. Sanderson products have been selected for use in the British royal palaces, "by appointment to HM Queen Elizabeth II. Suppliers of Wallpapers, Paints & Fabrics."

Schumacher Wallcoverings
79 Madison Avenue
New York, NY 10016
Telephone: 800-988-7775
Fax: 212-213-7848
Web site: www.fsco.com
E-mail: consumer@fsco.com

Schumacher Wallcoverings is a high-end designer-brand border and wallcovering manufacturer with fabric-driven patterns. Although widely distributed, interior designers often resort to a visit to Schumacher's New York showroom to view the collections. The Schumacher Wallcovering brand operates independently of its sister company brands, Gramercy, Greff (another designer brand), Village, and Waverly.

Seabrook Wallcoverings, Inc.
1325 Farmville Road
Memphis, TN 38122
Telephone: 800-238-9152
Fax: 901-320-3675

Seabrook Wallcoverings manages the design and manufacture of wallcovering collections under the Seabrook Designs brand name, available to consumers and designers nationwide. They publish Seabrook Journal twice annually for decorating retailers and interior designers, which provides tips, stories, and the introduction of new pattern collections.

Sunworthy Wallcoverings
195 Walker Drive
Brampton, Ontario
Canada LGT 3Z9
Telephone: 905-791-8788
Fax: 905-790-4883
Web site: www.sunworthy.com

Sunworthy wallcoverings are available in solid vinyl, vinyl coated, paintable, and faux finishes. They are widely distributed and popular with the do-it-yourself market. Sunworthy collections are distributed through Sunwall of America in Duluth, Georgia, and are available through most paint and paper stores, home centers, and retail outlets catering to home furnishings.

Village
79 Madison Avenue
New York, NY 10016
Telephone: 800-552-WALL
Fax: 212-213-7640

Village offers a full range of wallcoverings and borders in popular patterns. Half of the design collection is geared toward the bedroom, bath, and kitchen. Many have matching fabrics available. Village is widely distributed and can be found in most paint and paper shops, retail stores that cater to the home decorating market, and selected home centers.

Warner of London—
Distributed by Whittaker & Woods
5100 Highlands Parkway
Smyrna, GA 30082
Telephone: 800-395-8760
Fax: 770-432-6215

Warner of London offers traditional and transitional wallpapers. Some matching fabrics are available. Distribution is international.

Warner Wallcoverings/
The Warner Company
108 South Desplaines Street
Chicago, IL 60661
Telephone: 800-621-1143
Fax: 312-372-9584
Web site: www.thewarnerco@
worldnet.att.net

Warner Wallcoverings offers a good range of styles and types available through most paint and paper stores and home furnishing stores. Many of their borders are laser cut, creating a dimensional look when applied. New products include seasonal Softac adhesive borders, allowing for temporary holiday decor.

Waverly
79 Madison Avenue
New York, NY 10016
Telephone: 800-423-5881
Web site: www.decoratewaverly.com
E-mail: access via web site

Waverly offers a full range of wallcoverings and borders distributed nationwide in wallpaper stores, home centers, and retailers. In addition, a broad selection of coordinating Waverly fabrics and home fashions are sold through their company-owned Waverly Home stores.

Williamsburg by F. Schumacher & Co.
79 Madison Avenue
New York, NY 10016
Telephone: 800-446-9240
E-mail: consumer@fsco.com

A collection of Colonial Williamsburg reproduction prints with matching fabrics is available though Schumacher and marketed by Colonial Williamsburg, Virginia.

York Wallcoverings
750 Linden Avenue
P.O. Box 5166
York, PA 17405-5166
Telephone: 717-846-4456
Fax: 717-843-5624
International Fax: 717-851-0315

York Wallcoverings produces collections using all four of the printing methods described in this book, making for a wide range of patterns and prints. York wallcoverings are sophisticated, stylish, yet current with today's trends. They are widely distributed, available in most paint and paper stores, and home design retail stores.

Zoffany—Distributed by Whittaker & Woods
5100 Highlands Parkway
Smyrna, GA 30082
Telephone: 800-395-8760
Fax: 770-432-6215

Zoffany offers eighteenth- and nineteenth-century reproduction wallcoverings and fabrics. Available are wallpapers, vinyl wallcoverings, and handprints. Some patterns have matching fabrics. Zoffany is sold internationally.

Flooring Resources, Designers

Dennis Jenkins
Dennis Jenkins and Associates Interior Design
5813 South West 68th Street
Miami, FL 33143
(305) 665-6960
pp. 108–111

Ted Montgomery
Indiana Architecture and Design
477 Ten Stones Circle
Charlotte, Vermont 05445
(802) 425-7717
www.indiana-architecture.com
Specialties: Sustainability, solar energy,
intentional communities.
pp. 116–121

Dalia Berlin, ASID
3511 Greenleaf Circle
Hollywood, FL 33021
(954) 967-6576

Leonard A. Hall
Endurance Flooring Co., Inc.
18460 NE 2nd Ave.
Miami, FL 33179

Alan Vaughn
Alan Vaughn Studios
3961 N. Ivy Road, NE
Atlanta, GA 30342
(770) 457-0820
alanvaughn@mindspring.com

Desiree Caskill, ASID
Casa Mia Design
P. O. Box 140817
Coral Gables, Florida 33114
(305) 569-0529
casa-mia@msn.com

Joanne Hurd Kitchen and Bath Design
862 Washington Street
Gloucester, MA 01930
(978) 283-5105

Cushman and Beckstrom
P. O. Box 655
82 Park Street
Stowe, Vermont 05672
(802) 253-2169
Specialties: Architecture, Interiors, Planning

David Hill and Susan Fuller,
Contractors
RR #1 Box 65
Woodstock, VT 05071
(802) 457-3943
Fax: (802) 457-4117

Peggy Gowan, AIA
Jonathan Baily Associates
Dallas, Texas
(469) 227-3900
Fax: (469) 227-3901

Jeffrey Berkus, Architect
Santa Barbara, California
(805) 687-310

Blackstock Leather
13452 Kennedy Road
Stouffville, L4A 7X5 Canada
(800) 663-6657

Win Whittman, AIA
The Avatar Group
Austin, Texas
(512) 494-1548

Ann Sacks
8120 NE 33rd Drive
Portland, OR 97211
(800) 278-8453
www.annsacks.com

Alan Vaughn
Alan Vaughn Studios
3961 North Ivy Road, NE
Atlanta, GA 30342
(770) 457-0820

Walker Zanger
13190 Telfair Ave.
Sylmar, CA 91342
(818) 504-0235

Harris-Tarkett, Inc.
P. O. Box 300
Johnson City, TN 37605
(423) 928-3122

Michaelian & Kohlberg
578 Broadway, 2nd Fl.
New York, NY 10012
(212) 431-9009

Kentucky Wood Floors, Inc.
4200 Reservoir Ave.
Louisville, KY 40213
(502) 451-6024

Country Floors
8735 Melrose Ave.
Los Angeles, CA 90069
(213) 657-0510

Mafi Wide Plank Flooring
Schneegattern, Austria
in U.S.A.: (804) 754-7181

Flooring Resources

A & M Wood Specialty
358 Eagle Street N.
Cambridge, ON N3H 5M2
(800) 265-2759
www.amwoodinc.com

A. E. Sampson & Son
P. O. Box 1010,
171 Camden Road
Warren, ME 04864
Phone: (207) 273-4000
Fax: (207) 273-4006
ddlewis@msn.com

ADI Corp.
5000 Nicholson Court
Bethesda, MD 20895
Phone: (301) 468-6856
Fax: (301) 468-0562
Marble and granite flooring

Aged Woods
147 West Philadelphia Street
York, PA 17403
Phone: (800) 233-9307
Fax: (717) 843-8104

Albany Woodworks
P. O. Box 729
Albany, LA 70711-0729
Phone: (225) 567-1155
Fax: (225) 567-5150
www.albanywoodworks.com

American Olean Tile Company
Box 271
Lansdale, PA 19446-0271
(215) 855-1111

American Rug Craftsmen
3090 Sugar Valley Rd. N.W.
Sugar Valley, GA 30746-5166
(800)-553-1734
AMS Imports Area Rugs

23 Ash Lane
Amherst, MA 01002
Phone: (800) 648-1816
Fax: (413) 256-0434
www.amsimports.com
Anderson Hardwood Floors
P. O. Box 1155
Clinton, SC 29325
Phone: (864) 833-6250
Fax: (864) 833-6664
www.andersonfloors.com

Ann Sacks
8120 NE Thirty-Third Drive
Portland, OR 97211
Phone: (503) 281-7751
Fax: (503) 287-8807
www.annsacks.com

Antiquarian Traders
9031 W. Olympic Boulevard
Beverly Hills, CA 90211-3541
Phone: (310) 247-3900
Fax: (310) 247-8864
www.antiquariantraders.com

Antique Woods and Colonial Restorations
1273 Reading Avenue
Boyertown, PA 19512
Phone: (888) 261-4284
www.vintagewoods.com

Architectural Timber & Millwork
49 Mount Warner Road
Hadley, MA 01035-0719
Phone: (413) 586-3045
Fax: (413) 586-3046

Armstrong World Industries
P. O. Box 3001
Lancaster, PA 17604
Phone: (717) 397-0611
ArtWorks Studio
337 Hayhne Ave. S.W.

Aiken, SC 29801
Phone: (803) 643-8335
Fax: (803) 643-8335
Floorcloths

Asia Minor Carpets
236 Fifth Avenue, 2nd Fl.
New York, NY 10001
Phone: (212) 447-9066
Fax: (212) 447-1879
Atlanta Oriental Rug Restoration
131 Bradford Street N.W.
Gainesville, GA 30501
Phone: (800) 926-7847
Fax: (770) 536-2228
rugray@mindspring.com

Augusta Lumber Co.
567 N. Charlotte Avenue
Waynesboro, VA 22980
Phone: (540) 946-9150
Fax: (540) 946-9168
www.comclin.net/augustalumber

Authentic Pine Floors
4042 Highway 42,
P. O. Box 206
Locust Grove, GA 30248
(770) 957-6-38
www.authenticpinefloors.com

Authentic Wood Floors
P. O. Box 153
Glen Rock, PA 17327
Phone: (717) 428-0904
Fax: (717) 428-0464

Award Hardwood Floors
401 N. 72nd Avenue
Wausau, WI 54401
Phone: (715) 849-8080
Fax: (715) 849-8081

Azrock Commercial Flooring
P. O. Box 354
Florence, AL 35631-0354
Phone: (800) 877-8455
Fax: (256) 766-3381
www.domco.com
A Division of Domco Inc.

Bamboo Flooring International
20950 Currier Road
Walnut, CA 91789
Phone: (800) 827-9261
Fax: (909) 594-6938
www.bamboo-flooring.com

Bangor Cork Company
William and D Street
Pen Argyl, PA 18072
(215) 863-9041

Barn Stormers
RR 1, Box 566
West Lebanon, ME 04027
(207) 658-9000

Barnes Lumber Manufacturing
P. O. Box 1383
Statesboro, GA 30459
Phone: (912) 768-8875
Fax: (912) 764-8713
www.barneslumber.com

Birger Juell, Ltd.
1337 Merchandise Mart
Chicago, IL 60654
Phone: (312) 464-9663
Fax: (312) 464-9664
Wood floors

Bloomsburg Carpet Industries
919 Third Avenue
New York, NY 10022
(212) 688-7447

BM Barnsiding
562 Rt. 17M
Monroe, NY 10950
Phone: (800) 499-0444
Fax: (914) 783-9471
bmbarn@frontiernet.net

Braid-Aid
466 Washington Street
Pembroke, MA 02359
(617) 826-6091

Brintons Carpets (USA) Limited
E-240 Route 4
Paramus, NJ 07652
(201) 368-0080

Broad-Axe Beam Co.
1320 Lee Roadz
Guilford, VT
Phone: (802) 257-0064
Fax: (802) 257-0064

Bruce Hardwood Floors
16803 Dallas Parkway
Addison, TX 75001
Phone: (800) 722-4647
Fax: (214) 887-2234
www.brucehardwoodfloors.com

Buckingham-Virginia Slate Corp.
P. O. Box 8
Arvonia, VA 23004-0008
Phone: (804) 581-1131
Fax: (804) 581-1130

Carlisle Restoration Lumber
1676 Route 9
Stoddard, NH 03464
Phone: (800) 595-9663
Fax: (603) 446-3540
www.wideplankflooring.com

Carpet and Rug Institute
P. O. Box 2048
Dalton, GA 30722-2048
Phone: (800) 882-8846
Fax: (706) 278-8835
www.carpet-rug.com

Centre Mills Antique Floors
P. O. Box 16
Aspers, PA 17304
Phone: (717) 334-0249
Fax: (717) 334-6223
www.igateway.com/mall/homeimp/wood/index

Charles R. Stock/V'Soske.
2400 Market Street
Philadelphia, PA 19103
(215) 568-3448
Carpets

Chestnut Specialists, Inc.
400 Harwinton Avenue
Plymouth, CT 06782
Phone: (860) 283-4209
Fax: (860) 283-4209
www.chestnutspec.com

Chestnut Woodworking & Antique Flooring Co.
P. O. Box 204
West Cornwall, CT 06796
Phone: (860) 672-4300
Fax: (860) 672-2441
www.chestnutwoodworking.com

Classic Revivals
1 Design Centter Place, Suite 545
Boston, MA 02210
Phone: (617) 574-9030
Fax: (617) 574-9027
Carpets

Columbia Forest Products
222 S.W. Columbia Street, Suite 1575
Portland, OR 97201-1575
Phone: (800) 547-4261
Fax: (503) 224-5294
www.columbiaproducts.com

Columbia Trading Company
547 S.W. Gaines Street
Portland, OR 97201
Phone: (888) 326-3477
Fax: (503) 279-8793
www.oregonlive.com/sites/columbiatrading

Congoleum Corporation
3705 Quakerbridge Road
P. O. Box 3172
Mercerville, NJ 08619-0127
Phone: (609) 584-3000
Fax: (609) 584-3518
www.congoleum.com

Conklin's Authentic Antique Barnwood &
Hand Hewn Beams
RD 1, Box 70
Butterfield Road
Susquehanna, PA 18847
Phone: (570) 465-3832
Fax: (570) 465-3835

www.conklinsbarnwood.com
Cordts Flooring Company
840 Lyle Court
Peekskill, NY 10566
Phone: (914) 737-8201
Fax: (914) 737-8201

Cork America
5657 Santa Monica Boulevard
Los Angeles, CA 90038
Phone: (213) 469-3228
Fax: (213) 465-5866

Costikyan Carpets
28-13 14th Street
Long Island City, NY 11102
(800) 247-7847

Cottage Interiors
396 Main St.
Bar Harbor, ME 04609-1511
Phone: (207) 288-5614
Fax: (207) 288-5421
www.cottageinteriors.com
Rugs

Country Braid House
462 Main St.
Tilton, NH 03276
Phone: (603) 286-4511
Fax: (603) 286-4155
www.countrybraidhouse.com

Country Floors, Inc.
15 East 16th Street
New York, NY 10003
(212) 627-8300

Country Settings
3305 W. Fourth Avenue
Belle, WV 25015
Phone: (304) 925-3863
Fax: (304) 925-3303

www.countrysettings.com

Country Wood Products
656 Fourth Street
Audubon, MN 56511
Phone: (218) 439-3385
Fax: (218) 439-3771

Couristan
919 Third Avenue
New York, NY 10022
(212) 371-4200

CPN
705 Moore Station Industrial Park
Prospect Park, PA 19076
Phone: (800) 437-3233
Fax: (610) 534-2285
www.cpninc.com
Underlayments, radiant heat

Craft House Inn Design Studio
S. England Street
Williamsburg, VA 23187
Phone: (757) 220-7503
Fax: (757) 221-8790

Craftsman Lumber Company
436 Main Street
Groton, MA 01450-0222
Phone: (978) 448-5621
Fax: (978) 448-2754
www.craftsmanlumber.com

Craftsman Style
1453 Fourth Street
Santa Monica, CA 90401
Phone: (310) 393-1468
Fax: (310) 393-5359
Carpets

Creative Tile Marketing
12323 S.W. 55th Street
Building 1000, Suite 1009-1010
Fort Lauderdale, FL 33330
Phone: (305) 858-8242
Fax: (305) 858-9926

Crossville Ceramics Co.
P. O. Box 1168
Crossville, TN 38557
Phone: (931) 484-2110
Fax: (931) 484-8418
www.crossville-ceramics.com

Daltile
7834 Hawn Freeway
P. O. Box 170130
Dallas, TX 75217
Phone: (800) 933-8453
Fax: (214) 309-4457
www.daltile.com

Design Materials
241 S. 55th St.
Kansas City, KS 66106
Phone: (913) 342-9796
Fax: (913) 342-9826
Natural fiber floor coverings

Designs in Tile
P. O. Box 358
Mount Shasta, CA 96067
Phone: (530) 926-2629
Fax: (530) 926-6467
www.designsintile.com

DLW Flooring Systems
Represented by Anderson, Dewald and
Associates
2750 Northaven, Suite 120
Dallas, TX 75229
(414) 247-4955
Linoleum

Domko Inc.
1001 Yamaska, Dept. TH1197
E. Farnham, Quebec J2N-1J7
(514) 293-3173

Duluth Timber Company
P. O. Box 16717
Duluth, MN 55816
Phone: (218) 727-2145
Fax: (218) 727-0393
www.duluthtimber.com

Dynamic Laser Applications
4704 Ecton Drive
Marietta, GA 30066
Phone: (770) 924-4998
Fax: (770) 926-5122

Eaton Hill Textile Works
334 Jake Martin Rd.
Marshfield, VT 05658
(802) 426-3733
ktsmith@connriver.net

Echeguren Slate
1495 Illinois Street
San Francisco, CA 94107
Phone: (800) 992-0701
Fax: (415) 206-9353
www.echeguren.com

Edward Molina Designs
196 Selleck Street
Stamford, CT 06902
(203) 967-9445
Carpets

Endicott Clay Products
Box 17
Fairbury, NE 68352
Phone: (402) 729-3315
Fax: (402) 729-5804

Environmental Design
908 S. E. 15th Street
Forest Lake, MN 55025
Phone: (612) 464-6190
Fax: (612) 464-6191

Epro, Inc.
156 E. Broadway
Westerville, OH 43081
Phone: (614) 882-6990
Fax: (614) 882-4210
One-of-a-kind ceramic tile

Esquire Ceramic Tile
300 International Boulevard
Clarksville, TN 37040
Phone: (800) 256-7924
Fax: (931) 647-9934
esquire@gish.com

European Treasures
72 N. Main Street
Hudson, OH 44236
(216) 656-4390

Family Heirloom Weavers
775 Meadowview Drive
Red Lion, PA 17356
Phone: (717) 246-2431
Fax: (717) 246-7439
www.familyheirloomweavers.com
Firebird Industries Ltd.
366 Hord Street
New Orleans, LA 70123
Phone: (504) 733-8204
Fax: (504) 733-8261
Ceramic tile

Floor Cloths of Arizona
527 W. Lawrence Lane
Phoenix, AZ 85021
(602) 371-9300
www.floorclothsofarizona.com

Florida Tile Industries
P. O. Box 447
Lakeland, FL 33802
Phone: (941) 687-7171
Fax: (941) 284-4007
www.fltile.com

Forbo Industries
Maplewood Drive
Hazelton, PA 18201
Phone: (800) 342-0604
Fax: (570) 450-0258
www.forbo-industries.com

Fulper Tile
34 W. Ferry Street
New Hope. PA 19067
Phone: (215) 862-3358
Fax: (215) 862-1318
fulpertile@aol.com

Good and Company
Salzburg Square, Route 101
Amherst, NH 03031
(603) 672-0490
Floorcloths

Goodwin Heart Pine Company
106 S.W. 109th Place
Micanopy, FL 32667
Phone: (352) 466-0339
Fax: (352) 466-0608
www.heartpine.com
goodwin@heartpine.com

Grigsby/Hallman Studio
1322 West Broad Street
Richmond, VA 23220
(804) 353-3738
Floorcloths, stenciling

Grill Works
1609 Halbur Road
Marshall, MN 56258
Phone: (800) 347-4745
Fax: (507) 532-3526
www.grillworks.com
Hardwood registers

H.K. Hardwoods
195 Libert Street
Brockton, MA 02401
Phone: (800) 530-0622
Fax: (508) 588-4698

Handwoven
6818 54th Avenue, N.E.
Seattle, WA 98115
(206) 524-9058
Rag rugs

Hardwood Council
P. O. Box 525
Oakmont, PA 15139
(412) 281-4980

Hardwood Information Center
100 First Avenue, Suite 525
Pittsburgh, PA 15222
Phone: (412) 323-9320
Fax: (412) 323-9334
www.hardwood.org

Harris-Tarkett
2225 Eddie Williams Road
Johnson City, TN 37601-2872
Phone: (423) 928-3122
Fax: (423) 928-9445
www.harristarkett.com
Solid, engineered, and laminate wood
flooring

Hartco Wood Flooring
565 Hartco Drive
Oneida, NY 37841
Phone: (800) 442-7826
Fax: (423) 569-9031
www.hartcoflooring.com

Heartwood Lumber Company
5801 Rhodes Avenue
New Orleans, LA 70131
Phone: (504) 394-6925
Fax: (504) 394-3013

Heirloom Rugs
28 Harlem Street
Rumford, RI 02916
(401) 438-5672

Heritage Rugs
R.D.1, Box 404
Lahaska, PA 18931
(215) 794-7229
Rag rugs

Hilltop Slate
P. O. Box 201, Rte. 22A
Middle Granville, NY 12849
(518) 642-1220

Historic Floors of Oshkosh
911 East Main Street
Winneconne, WI 54986
Phone: (920) 582-9977
Fax: (920) 582-9971
info@historicfloors.com

Historical Hand Painted Tile
2104 E. Seventh Avenue
Tampa, FL 33605
Phone: (813) 247-6817
Fax: (813) 242-8021

Hoboken Floors
70 Demarest Drive
Wayne, NJ
(800) 222-1068

Dimension Lumber & Milling
517 Stagg Street
Brooklyn, NY 11237
Phone: (718) 497-1680
Fax: (718) 366-6531

Intarsia, Inc.
1851 Cypress Lake Drive, Suite B
Orlando, FL 32837
Phone: (407) 859-5800
Fax: (407) 859-7555

Interceramic, USA
2333 S. Jupiter Road
Garland, TX 75041
Phone: (800) 496-8453
Fax: (214) 503-5575
www.interceramicsusa.com

Interior Vision in the Craftsman Style
P. O. Box 867
Port Townsend, WA 98368
Phone: (888) 385-3161
Fax: (360) 385-4874

International Floors of America, Inc.
3355 Lenox Road, N.E., Suite 270
Atlanta, GA 30326
Phone: (404) 846-1112
Fax: (404) 846-1114
Centiva@aol.com

International Hardwood Flooring
7400 Edmund Street
Philadelphia, PA 19136
Phone: (800) 338-7481
Fax: (215) 624-4577

Isabel O'Neil Studio and Foundation
177 East 87th Street
New York, NY 10022
(212) 751-6414
Floorcloths, stenciling

J. L. Powell & Co
600 S. Madison Street
Whiteville, NC 28472
Phone: (800) 227-2007
Fax: (919) 642-3164

J.R. Burrows and Company
P. O. Box 522
Rockland, MA 02370
Phone: (781) 982-1812
Fax: (781) 982-1636
www.burrows.com
merchant@burrows.com
carpets

Janos P. Spitzer Flooring Company
44 West 22nd Street
New York, NY 10010
(212) 627-1818

John Sherman
P. O. Box 152
West Pawlet, VT 05775
(802) 645-9828
Floorcloths

Kahrs International Inc.
951 Mariners Island Boulevard
San Mateo, CA 94404
(800) 800-5247
www.kahrs.com

Karastan Bigelow
P. O. Box 3089
Greenville, SC 29602
(803) 299-2000

Kentile Floors
58 Second Avenue
New York, NY 11215
(718) 768-9500

Kentucky Wood Floors
P. O. Box 33276
Louisville, KY 40232
Phone: (800) 235-5235
Fax: (502) 451-6027
www.kentuckywood.com

Kitchens Unique, Inc. by Lois
P. O. Box 689
259 Main St.
Chester, NJ 07930
Phone: (908) 879-6473
Fax: (908) 879-2446

L'esperance Tileworks
240 Sheridan Avenue
Albany, NY 12210
(518) 465-5586

Lacey-Champion Carpets
Box 216
Fairmount, GA 30139
(404) 337-5355

Langhorne Carpet Co.
P. O. Box 7175
201 W. Lincoln Highway
Penndel, PA 19047-0824
Phone: (215) 757-5155
Fax: (215) 757-2212

Launstein Hardwood Products
384 Every Road
Mason, MI 48854
Phone: (517) 676-1133
Fax: (517) 676-6379

Liberty Cedar
535 Libert Lane
West Kingston, RI 02892
Phone: (800) 882-3327
Fax: (401) 789-0320
lc@libert-cedar.com

Linden Lumber
P. O. Drawer 480369
Highway 43N
Linden, AL 36748
Phone: (334) 295-8751
Fax: (334) 295-8088

Linoleum City
5657 Santa Monica Boulevard
Hollywood, CA 90038
(213) 469-0063

Lizzie and Charlie's Rag Rugs
210 E. Bullion Avenue
Marysvale, UT 84750
(801) 326-4213
www.marysvale.org

London Tile Co.
65 Walnut Street
New London, OH 44851
Phone: (888) 757-1551
Fax: (419) 929-1552

Longwood Restoration
330 Midland Place
Lexington, KY 40505
Phone: (800) 225-7857
Fax: (606) 299-8205

M. L. Condon Company
254 Ferris Avenue
White Plains, NY 10603
Phone: (914) 946-4111
Fax: (914) 946-3779
Lumber and millwork

Manhattan Art & Antiques Center
1050 Second Avenue
New York, NY 10022
Phone: (212) 355-4400
Fax: (212) 355-4403
www.the_maac.com

Mannington
P. O. Box 30, Route 45
Salem, NJ 08079-0030
Phone: (856) 935-3000
Fax: (856) 339-5948
www.mannington.com

Marblelife
805 W. N. Carrier Parkway
Suite 220
Grand Prairie, TX 75050
Phone: (800) 627-4569
Fax: (972) 623-0220
www.marblelife.com

Mark Inc.
323 Railroad Avenue
Greenwich, CT 06830
Phone: (800) 227-0927
Fax: (203) 861-0197
Carpets

Marlborough Country Barn
N. Main Street
Marlborough, CT 06447
Phone: (800) 852-8893
Fax: (860) 295-7424
Rugs

Mary Moross Studios
122 Chambers Street
New York, NY 10007
Phone: (212) 571-0437
Fax: (212) 267-6594
Floorcloths

Mcintyre Tile Co.
55 W. Grantt Street
Healdsburg, CA 95448
Phone: (707) 433-8866
Fax: (707) 433-0548
www.mcintyre-tile.com

Mexican Handcrafted Tile/MC Designs
7595 Carroll Rd.
San Diego, CA 92121
Phone: (858) 689-9596
Fax: (858) 689-9597

Michael FitzSimmons Decorative Arts
311 W. Superior Street
Chicago, IL 60610
Phone: (312) 787-0496
Fax: (312) 787-6343

Michaelian & Kohlberg
578 Broadway, 2nd Fl.
New York, NY 10012
Phone: (212) 431-9009
Fax: (212) 431-9077
Carpets

Milliken Contract Carpeting
P. O. Box 2956
La Grange, GA 30241
(404) 883-5511

Milton W. Bosley Co.
P. O. Box 576
Glen Burnie, MD 21061
Phone: (800) 638-5010
Fax: (410) 553-1575
mbosley@clark.net
Wood moldings

Mintec Corp.
100 E. Pennsylvania Avenue, Suite 210
Towson, MD 21286
Phone: (888) 9-MINTEC
Fax: (410) 296-6693
www.bamtex.com
Bamboo flooring

Moravian Pottery and Tile Works
Swamp Road
Doylestown, PA 18901
(215) 345-6722

Mountain Lumber
P. O. Box 289
Ruckersville, VA 22968
(800) 445-2671
www.mountainlumber.com

Nature's Loom
32 E. 31st Street
New York, NY 10016
Phone: (800) 365-2002
Fax: (212) 213-8414
www.naturesloom.com

New England Hardwood Supply Co. Inc.
100 Taylor Street
Littleton, MA 01460
Phone: (800) 540-8683
Fax: (978) 486-9703

New England Wholesale Hardwoods
Rt. 82 S, Box 534
Pine Plains, NY 12567-0534
Phone: (518) 398-9663
Fax: (518) 398-9666
www.floorings.com

NOFMA
P. O. Box 3009
Memphis, TN 38173
Phone: (901) 526-5016
Fax: (901) 526-7022
www.nofma.org
Trade organization for hardwood flooring
manufacturers

Nordic American Corp.
15 Plantation Drive
Atlanta, GA 30324
Phone: (800) 242-8160
Fax: (404) 250-9531
Engineered flooring

North American Slate
50 Columbus St.
Granville, NY 12832
Phone: (518) 642-1702
Fax: (518) 642-3255
nas99slate@aol.com

Old World Restorations
7901 Thayer Drive
Fort Smith, AR 72908
(501) 646-1328
Slate floor repair

Ould Colony Artisans
169 Albert Ave.
Cranston, RI 02905-3811
Phone: (800) 414-7906
Fax: (401) 781-0775
Floorcloths

Paris Ceramics (USA) Inc.
151 Greenwich Avenue
Greenwich, CT 06830
Phone: (203) 552-9658
Fax: (203) 552-9655

Parquet de France
54 Byram Road
Point Pleasant, PA 18950-0156
Phone: (215) 297-5255
Fax: (215) 297-5255
Importers of French parquet

Past Perfect
1212 Washington Street
Holliston, MA 01746
Phone: (508) 429-7752
Fax: (508) 429-5997
viatorcomm@aol.com
Floorcloths

Patina Woods Company
3563 New Franklin Road
Chambersburg, PA 17201
(717) 264-8009

Patterson, Flynn & Martin
979 Third Avenue
New York, NY 10022
Phone: (212) 688-7700
Fax: (212) 826-6740
Rugs and carpeting

PED Products Company
P. O. Box 321
Springfield, PA 19064
(215) 328-4950
Linoleum

Peerless Imported Rugs
3028 North Lincoln Avenue
Chicago, IL 60657
(800) 621-6573

Pennsylvannia Woven Carpet Mills
401 East Allegheney Avenue
Philadelphia, PA 19134
(610) 215-5833

Flooring Resources, *continued*

Pergo/ Perstop Flooring, Inc.
P. O. Box 1775
Horsham, PA 19044
(800) 337-3746
www.pergo.com

Persnickety
P. O. Box 458
776 East Walker Road
Great Falls, VA 22066
(703) 450-7150
Rag and hooked rugs

Pewabic Pottery
10125 E. Jefferrson Avenue
Detroit, MI 48214
Phone: (313) 822-0954
Fax: (313) 822-6266
www.pewabic.com

Piedmont Hardwood Flooring
P. O. Box 3070
Macon, GA 31205
Phone: (888) 791-0155
Fax: (912) 781-7288

Plaza Hardwood
219 W. Manhattan Avenue
Santa Fe, NM 87501
Phone: (800) 662-6306
Fax: (505) 992-8766
www.plzfloor.com

Premier Wood Floors
16803 Dallas Parkway
Dallas, TX 75248
(800) 588-1707

Premium Hardwood Floors & Supplies Inc.
121 31st Street (corner of 3rd Avenue)
Brooklyn, NY 11232
Phone: (718) 369-3141
Fax: (718) 369-3139
www.premium-floors.com/pwf
pwf@premium-floors.com

Quality Woods
95 Bartley Road
Flanders, NJ 07034
Phone: (973) 584-7554
Fax: (973) 584-3875
teakwood1@sprynet.com

Rare Earth Hardwoods
6778 E. Traverse Highway
Traverse City, MI 49684
Phone: (800) 968-0074
Fax: (800) 968-0094

Rastetter Woolen Mill
5802 State Route 39
Millersburg, OH 44654
(216) 674-2103

Renaissance Tile & Marble
P. O. Box 412
Cherry Valley, NY 13320
Phone: (607) 264-8474
Fax: (607) 264-8474
www.tilemarbleandgranite.com

Riley Design
P. O. Box 626
Croton Falls, NY 10519-0626
(914) 277-0860
Floorcloths

Robbins Brothers
919 Third Avenue
New York, NY 10022
(212) 421-1050
Carpets

Robbins Hardwood Flooring
4785 Eastern Avenue
Cincinnati, OH 45226
(800) 733-3309
www.robbinsflooring.com

Rosecore Carpets
979 Third Avenue
New York, NY 10022
(212) 421-7272

Rustigian Rugs
1 Governor Street
Providence, RI 02906
(401) 751-5100

Sandy Pond Hardwoods
921-A Lancaster Pike
Quarryville, PA 17566
Phone: (800) 546-9663
Fax: (717) 284-5739
www.figuredhardwoods.com

Saxony Carpet Company
979 Third Avenue
New York, NY 10022
(212) 755-7100

Scalamandre
950 Third Avenue
New York, NY 10022
(212) 980-3888
Carpets

Schumacher
79 Madison Avenue
New York, NY 10016
(800) 332-3384
Carpets

Schumacher and Company
938 Third Avenue
New York, NY 10022
(212) 415-3900

Seneca Tiles
7100 S. Country Road, Suite 23
Attica, OH 44807
Phone: (800) 426-4335
Fax: (419) 426-1735

Shaw Rugs
P. O. Drawer 2128
Dalton, GA 30722-2128
(800) 282-SHAW

Sheldon Slate Products Co. Inc.
Fox Road
Middle Granville, NY 12849
Phone: (518) 642-1280
Fax: (518) 642-9085
www.sheldonslate.com

Shep Brown Associates
24 Cummings Park
Woburn, MA 01801
Phone: (617) 935-8080
Fax: (617) 935-2090
www.shepbrownassociates.com
Tile and stone

Smith & Fong
650-872-1184
Plyboo

Southeastern Lumber Manufacturers
Association
P. O. Box 1788
Forest Park, GA 30051-1788
Phone: (404) 361-1445
Fax: (404) 361-5963

Special Effects by Sue
8113 Oakbrook Lane, S.W.
Tacoma, WA 98498
(206) 582-7821
Floorcloths

Stark Carpet
979 Third Avenue
New York, NY 10022
Phone: (212) 752-9000
Fax: (212) 758-4342
www.starkcarpet.com

Stone Tech
24-16 Queens Plaza S.
Long Island City, NY 11101
Phone: (718) 784-4646
Fax: (718) 784-1580
stonetech@aol.com

Structural Slate Co.
222 E. Main St.
P. O. Box 187
Pen Argyl, PA 18072
Phone: (800) 677-5283
Fax: (610) 863-7016
www.structuralslate.com

Sturbridge Yankee Workshop
Blueberry Road
Westbrook, ME 04092
Phone: (800) 343-1144

Summitville Tiles
P. O. Box 73
Summitville, OH 43962
Phone: (330) 223-1511
Fax: (330) 223-1414
www.summitville.com

Superior Water-Logged Lumber Co.
2200 E. Lake Shore Drive
Ashland, WI 54806
Phone: (715) 685-9663
Fax: (715) 685-9620
www.oldlogs.com

Sylvan Brandt
651 E. Main St.
Lititz, PA 17543
Phone: (717) 626-4520
Fax: (717) 626-5867
www.sylvanbrandt.com

Tarkett Inc.
1139 Lehigh Avenue
Whitehall, PA 18052
(800) 367-8275
www.tarkettna.com

Terra Designs
241 East Blackwell Street
Dover, NJ 07801
(201) 539-2999
Tile

Terrazzo & Marble Supply Companies
5700 S. Hamilton
Chicago, IL 60636
Phone: (773) 471-0700
Fax: (773) 471-5010

The Carpet and Rug Institute
P. O. Box 2048
Dalton, GA 30722
Phone: (800) 882-8846
Fax: (706) 278-8835

The Gazebo of New York
660 Madison Avenue
New York, NY 10021
(212) 832-7077
Rag, braided, and hooked rugs

The Joinery Company
P. O. Box 518
Tarboro, NC 27886
(252) 823-3306

The Persian Carpet
5634 Chapel Hill Boulevard
Durham, NC 27707
Phone: (800) 333-1801
Fax: (919) 439-3529

The Roof Tile & Slate Co.
1209 Carrol
Carollton, TX 75006
Phone: (800) 446-0220
Fax: (972) 242-1923
www.rts.com

The Woods Co.
5045 Kansas Avenue
Chambersburg, PA 17201
Phone: (717) 263-6524
Fax: (717) 263-9346

Thomas D. Osborn
1421 Northampton Street
Holyoke, MA 01040
Phone: (413) 532-9034
Fax: (413) 532-0241
Marquetry and inlaid floors

Tile Restoration Center
3511 Interkae Avenue N.
Seattle, WA 98103
Phone: (206) 633-4866
Fax: (206) 633-3489
www.tilerestorationcenter.com

Tile Showcase
291 Arsenal Street
Watertown, MA 02172
Phone: (617) 926-1100
Fax: (617) 926-9714

Tilecera
300 International Boulevard
Clarksville, TN 37040
Phone: (800) 782-8453
Fax: (931) 647-9934

U.S. Axminster
Box 877
East Union Extended
Greenville, MS 38702-0877
(601) 332-1581

U.S. Ceramic Tile Co.
10233 Sandyville Road, S.E.
East Sparta, OH 44626-9333
Phone: (330) 866-5531
Fax: (330) 866-5340
www.usceramictileco.com

Universal Flooring
14800 Quorum Drive, Suite 110
(972) 387-0867
Dallas, TX 75240

Vermont Structural Slate Co.
P. O. Box 98
3 Prospect Street
Fair Haven, VT 05743
Phone: (800) 343-1900
Fax: (802) 265-3865

Vintage Lumber and Construction
Company
9507 Woodsboro Road
Frederick, MD 21701
(301) 898-7859

Vintage Pine
P. O. Box 85
Prospect, VA 23960
Phone: (804) 248-9000
Fax: (804) 248-9409

Walker Zanger
8901 Bradley Avenue
Sun Valley, CA 91352
Phone: (818) 504-0235
Fax: (818) 504-2226
Tile and stone

Wilsonart International
2400 Wilson Place
P. O. Box 6110
Temple, TX 76503-6110
Phone: (800) 710-8846
Fax: (817) 778-2711
www.wilsonart.com
Laminates

Winterthur Museum, Garden, and Library
Kennett Pike
Winterthur, DE 19810
Phone: (800) 448-3883
Fax: (302) 888-4820
Carpets

Woodawrd & Greenstein/Woodard Weave
506 E. 74th Street, 5th Fl.
New York, NY 10021
Phone: (800) 332-7847
Fax: (212) 734-9665
wgantiques@aol.com

Woodhouse
P. O. Box 7336
Rocky Mount, NC 27804
Phone: (919) 977-7336
Fax: (919) 641-4477

World Class Floors
333 S.E. Second Avenue, Suite 168
Portland, OR 97214
Phone: (800) 547-6634
Fax: (503) 736-2566
www.contactintl.com

Yankee Exotic Woods
P. O. Box 211
Cornish, NH 03746
Phone: (603) 675-6206
Fax: (603) 675-6306

Yankee Pride
29 Parkside Circle
Braintree, MA 02184
(800) 848-7610

Yield House
P. O. Box 2525
Conway, NH 03818-2525
Phone: (800) 659-0206
Fax: (603) 447-1717

Additional Resources

Decorative Artists

Bopas, Inc.
Robert Grady
Gedes Paskauskas
30 Ipswich Street
Boston, MA 02215
Tel: (617) 236-4919
Fax: (617) 266-0725
page 4, 11, 12–19

Patti Bruce Decorative Art
4614 Kilanea Avenue, Suite 312
Honolulu, HI 96816
Tel/Fax: (808) 926-8866
page 107, 132–137

Charlene "Charley" Ayuso Cooper
FAUXFinish Studio, Inc.
700 Evans Creek Court
San Ramon, CA 94583
Tel: (925) 551-7732
Fax: (925) 833-0373
e-mail: FAUXCEO@aol.com
page 11, 20–27

Peter Brian Daly
Artscope Enterprizes
2961 Columbia Street #16
San Diego, CA 92103
Tel: (619) 230-9138
page 92–97

Helen R. Doane
653 Main Street
Harwich, MA 02645
Tel: (508) 432-5548
page 53, 54–61

Jeff Entner
577A State Road
Vineyard Haven, MA 02568
Tel: (508) 693-5845
page 11, 28–35

Joe Fenzl
Decorative Arts of Los Angeles
1618 1/2 Euclid Street
Santa Monica, CA 90404
Tel/Fax: (310) 396-8636
page 11, 36–43

Robert A. Fischer
Palm Springs, CA 92264
Represented by Patrick Sheehan
(See Additional Resources listing)
page 98–105

Robert Grady
Bopas, Inc.
30 Ipswich Street
Boston, MA 02215
Tel: (617) 236-4919
Fax: (617) 266-0725
page 4, 12–19

Martin Alan Hirsch
Decorative Finishes Studio
1905 Bardstown Road
Louisville, KY 40205
Tel: (800) 598-FAUX (-3289)
Fax: (502) 473-1562
www.fauxfinish.com
page 11, 44–51

Suzanne Mastroluca
Impressions In Paint
1509 Alma Terrace
San Jose, CA 95125
Tel: (408) 286-4460
Fax: (408) 286-4112
page 53, 84–91

Kathy McDonald, Designer
5 N. 411 Harvest Lane
St. Charles, IL 60175
Tel/Fax: (630) 377-5167
page 53, 62–69

Julie Sims Messenger
Art Floorcloths
Tel: (781) 545-6569
page 107, 116–123

Michael Tyson Murphy
135 West 20th Street #400
New York, NY 10011
Tel: (212) 989-0180
Fax: (212) 989-0443
page 78–83

Mary Jo Parker O'Hearn
1636 77th Court
Elmwood Park, IL 60707
Tel: (708) 456-4065
page 107, 124–131

John Parsons
7 Seymour Street
Quincy, MA 02169
Tel: (617) 328-0155
page 53, 70–77

Gedes Paskauskas
Bopas, Inc.
30 Ipswich Street
Boston, MA 02215
Tel: (617) 236-4919
Fax: (617) 266-0725
page 4, 12–19

Leslie Ann Powers
European Stenciling, Trompe l'oeil & Murals
241 State Street
Guilford, CT 06437
Tel/Fax: (203) 453-9583
page 108–115

Dale Michaels Wade
625 Bridge Road
Eastham, MA 02642
Tel: (508) 255-1371
Fax: (508) 255-6328

Photo Credits

Graham Atkins-Hughes/Red Cover, 180 (right), 244 (bottom)

Paul Bardagy/Through the Lens Management, 169; 174; 185

Carolyn L. Bates, 163; 165; 177; 180 (left); 183 (middle right); 194 (left); 217 (left); 242; 243 (top)

Courtesy of Country Floors, 227 (top left)

Dietrich/Report Bilder-Dienst GmbH, 166; 209 (left)

Scott Dorrance, 161; 191 (top right & bottom left)

Christopher Drake/Red Cover, 240 (top right)

Hajo/Willig/Picture Press, 235 (left)

Courtesy of Harris-Tarkett, Inc., 179; 183 (top left);195 (bottom)

Hefe/Report Bilder-Dienst GmbH, 202

Winfried Heinze/Red Cover, 219 (top & bottom right)

Graham Henderson/Elizabeth Whiting & Associates, 229

Hoernisch/Report Bilder-Dienst GmbH, 207

Greg Hursley/Through the Lens Management, 167

Courtesy of Kentucky Wood Floors, 221

Mark Luscomb-Whyte/Elizabeth Whiting & Associates, 198

Courtesy of Mafi Wide Plank Flooring, 219 (top left)

Bruce Martin, 205 (left)

Courtesy of Michaelian & Kohlberg, 208, 209 (right)

Ivo Nörenberg/Picture Press, 235 (right)

Greg Premru/Joanne Hurd Kitchen Design, 205 (right)

Lanny Provo, 175; 194 (right); 195 (top); 236

Courtesy of Ann Sacks, 212

Peter A. Sellar, 237 (left)

Dennis Stone/Elizabeth Whiting & Associates, 197

Tim Street-Porter/www.beateworks.com, 173

Brian Vanden Brink, 170; 171; 172; 183 (top right, middle left, lower left & right); 187; 194 (middle); 219 (bottom left); 231; 239

Brian Vanden Brink/Berhard & Priestly, Architects, 217 (top right)

Brian Vanden Brink/Stephen Blatt Architects, 240 (bottom left)

Brian Vanden Brink/Rick Burt, Architect, 191 (bottom right); 241

Brian Vanden Brink/Tom Catalano, Architect, 240 (bottom right)

Brian Vanden Brink/Lo Yi Chan, Architect, 240 (top left)

Brian Vanden Brink/Drysdale Associates Interior Design, 171; 223 (right)

Brian Vanden Brink/Reiter & Reiter Architects, 191 (top left)

Brian Vanden Brink/Tom Rouselle, Architect, 217 (bottom right)

Brian Vanden Brink/Scholz & Barclay Architects 162; 223 (left)

Brian Vanden Brink/Scogin, Elam & Bray Architects, 191 (middle); 243 (bottom)

Brian Vanden Brink/Rob Whitten Architect, 244 (top)

Courtesy of Alan Vaughn Studios, 225

Courtesy of Walker Zanger, 203; 211; 227 (top right)

Paul Warchol, 237 (right)

Willig/Picture Press, 233; 245

Willig/Alberts/Picture Press, 186

Willig/Lichtenstein/Picture Press, 201

About the Authors

Liz Risney Manning is an interior designer and former training manager for a large paint and wallcovering company. She has conducting classes on how to use paint and wallcoverings, and has written many how-to brochures and video scripts on the subject. She currently works for an architectural/engineering firm.

Regina Cole has written extensively on architecture, interior design, and the history of the American decorative arts for both books and magazines. She is an editor-at-large at *Old-House Interiors* magazine, where she was a senior editor for many years. She often lectures on the subject of historic kitchen styles, with emphasis on their suitability for modern living. She also writes travel articles, political commentary, and poetry. She lives in Gloucester, Massachusetts.

Karen Aude is an arts writer and collage artist. Her articles have been published in several regional and national magazines and newspapers, and she is the author of *Heather Braginton-Smith*, a monograph on the work of the trompe l'oeil artist. Aude lives in Yarmouthport, Massachusetts, with her two feline companions, Bohditree and Sami.